Camping on Shabbat

How to: Build an Eruv, Bake Bread, go to the Toilet, and More...

Published by

Ben Tanny

rabbiben@travelingrabbi.com

Dedication

Dedicated to Dr. Howard Spielman. As a youth, in a *Shomer Shabbat* Scout Troop in Far Rockaway, NY, he earned Eagle Scout (highest scouting award in the USA) with four Palms, and the *NerTamid* (the Jewish scouting award). A Scout and Scouter for over 57 years, he has served as Scoutmaster of his *Shomer Shabbat* Troop 54 for over 26 years and has led his troop for 26 summers to Scout camps with a kosher dining hall. He was Wood Badge trained in 1987 and has staffed two 'Sabbath Observant' Wood Badge Courses. He has been to Philmont three times and has led a number of *ShomerShabbat* High Adventure Treks, including a 69-mile Horseback Trek in the Colorado Rockies, 100-mile Canoe Trek in the Adirondacks, and 150-mile Cycling Merit Badge and trek through the Catskill Mountains.

Thanks to Dr.Spielman, my family and I continue to have many opportunities to explore the outdoors while not compromising our Judaism. My years in scouting laid the foundations for my outdoor skills.

A special thank you...

Special thanks to my parents, Rabbi Chaim and PeshaTanny for supporting this project. My parents have long been advocates for the study of Torah and for taking time to spend in nature. On a nice summer's day you could find my father sitting by the lake reading from a pile of Torah books and my mother helping prepare a kosher meal at a Jewish Scouting campout. In the Tanny home, enjoying time in nature and maintaining a Jewish lifestyle are fully compatible.

The Mishkan (Tabernacle) was built by the Jewish People as they travelled through the desert from Egypt to Israel. (We Jews have been camping for a long time!) This movable sanctuary eventually found a permanent home in Jerusalem - the Beit HaMikdash (Holy Temple). The Mishkan was built so it could be taken apart and carried from place to place. Each large object had a ring in its corner, through which poles could be placed for carrying. The poles were only needed for carrying. Once the object was in place, the poles could be removed. Except for one item - the Aron (holy ark) which contained the Torah. Concerning the Aron the Torah tells us the poles must remain in place at all times, even when it was resting. One reason is the message that Torah, in its widest sense, must be able to go anywhere. Torah must accompany us, teach and inspire us, guide and light our path wherever we go.

This volume is extraordinary in that it acts like the poles of the Aron, allowing us to carry our observance of Torah to the most remote locations. And there is deep benefit to being in these locations - allowing us to appreciate God's beautiful world, and come to a deeper understanding of ourselves and our place in it.

I have not reviewed every Halachic decision in these pages - readers should always consult their rabbi. But I am amazed by the attention to detail this volume contains. And I think this work magnificently prepares a Jew for enjoying the harmony of nature while impressing every reader with the way in which our Torah has something deep to teach us at every moment in every place.

Rabbi Michael Whitman

Michael Whitman, Rabbi
AdathIsraelPoaleZedekAnsheiOzer of
Montreal CANADA

After the Maggid's death, his students gathered together and discussed the things their teacher had done. When it came to Rabbi SchneurZalman's turn, he questioned them "Do you know why your master went to the pond every day at dawn and stayed there for a while before coming home again?" They could not answer. Rabbi Zalman continued, "He was learning the song with which the frogs praise G-d. It takes a long time to learn that song."

Tales of the Hasidim- Early Masters, p. 111

Rabbi Shimon said, "The shade spread over us by these trees is so pleasant! We must crown this place with words of Torah."

Zohar, 2:127a

It is good to pray and dialogue with G-d in the field amongst the grass and trees. When a person prays in the field then all the plants and animals join in the prayer and help him or her giving strength to the prayer.

Rabbi Nachman of Bratslav

All that we see - the heaven, the earth, and all that fills it - all these things are the external garments of G-d.

RebbeShneurZalman of Liadi,*Tanya*, 42

Table of Contents

Halachic Disclaimer

Halacha is the Jewish code of law that outlines countless aspects of a person's life. It governs much of what we can and cannot do, from the moment we wake up in the morning until we retire at the end of the day. Even when we sleep, Halacha tells us how we should lie in bed.

Some Halachic rulings are black-and-white, and accepted by everyone operating in a Jewish framework that follows Halacha; for example: not eating pork. No Orthodox rabbi will ever permit eating pork under normal circumstances, because it is expressly forbidden by the Torah. Things get complicated when there is nothing explicit in the Torah pertaining to a specific matter, since the rabbis must draw their own Halachic conclusions based on their own interpretations of the text. Because of this, there are areas of Halacha where rabbis disagree with each other. It may be about something seemingly simple, like in what order a blessing should be recited. Or, it may be something with such serious implications as whether or not a particular person's conversion to Judaism is valid.

I want to be clear that in no way am I advising you to follow one way or another with regards to anything in this book. What I do or say in the book, may or may not even entirely reflect my personal view of a Halachic approach to a situation. Even if it did at the time, things may have since changed. Please do not infer any Halachic rulings. Be sure to consult your local rabbi if you are unsure about something.

You may notice as you read that I do not list many sources or discussions between rabbis with regards to Halachic outcomes. My intention for this book is that it serve as a practical guide for people wanting to camp on Shabbat. I do not intend for it to be learned as a theoretical halachic piece of work where individuals can debate various sides of which position we follow with regards to particularities. Thus said, even if you have no intention of camping on Shabbat, or ever camping at all, you are still welcome to enjoy the content in this book from a Torah study perspective.

Prologue

We made it to our camp site minutes before sunset and I began frantically putting up my tent. This caused some discomfort amongst the porters because it is their job to put up and take down the tents. They kept trying to get me to stop helping them. With a 99.7% language-barrier problem - I, not speaking Swahili and they, not speaking English - I was not going to start explaining Shabbat and its logistical implications. I needed the tent erected and all my stuff set up for Shabbat. I had lots of stuff to do, like inflating an air mattress, tearing some toilet paper, and so on. With two minutes to sunset, I had everything sorted - or, at least, I thought I did!

As I lay in my tent, catching my breath from exerting myself in the already thin air, I experienced a sharp, annoying pain on my leg. Now, I say "on" my leg and not "in" my leg because it was coming from something outside of me. During the moment I spent processing the sensation, I felt an identical sensation on my other leg, and then a third...a fourth...I jumped up and scanned floor of the tent carefully and quickly.

"Goodness," I said, as I grabbed a cloth and began whacking the dozen or so fire ants that had crawled over the air mattress and were attempting to get into my sleeping bag. While setting things up in the tent, I had left the door open for a few minutes, and the ants had invaded. I continued to kill them, frantically, one by one.

"Out," I hissed at them. "Be quick or you'll be quickly squished."

All ants had to be out of the tent or dead before Shabbat. I knew some of them were hiding and buying time. Once Shabbat arrived, I would no longer be able to switch on a light to search for them, nor kill them once found.

"Hot water for you, sir," said a porter, as he placed a basin in front of my tent.

"What?" I said, surprised. "Hot water?"

"Yes," explained the porter. "Washing for you, sir."

Wow, I thought. This was the first time after a long day of hiking that I got hot water to wash up with. I was also very happy because it's a mitzvah to shower or bathe on Friday in honor of Shabbat. Perhaps nowadays we don't think much about taking a shower or bath, but a few hundred years ago, one had to go to a bathhouse and pay money. Washing up was a once-a-month activity, or perhaps a once-a-week event, if you were rich. If one could not wash his whole body before Shabbat, he should at least wash his hands and feet.

I quickly pulled off my socks and shirt, and enjoyed the water for some sixty seconds as I washed my face, hands, feet, and upper body. I felt the warm water wash over me and savored the sensations. It's in moments like these that I feel like I'm doing something special for Shabbat. Taking a shower is such a normal, routine event that most of us are barely aware of what we're doing, let alone being present to the fact that we may be doing something for honoring the Shabbat. But when we change from what we are accustomed to, we usually become present, conscious that we are doing something different, operating from a place other than that which we had been used to.

Tired from the day's hike, I collapsed. Though I could not relax for long; I had to pray while I still had some daylight and was able to read from my prayer book. I found the correct page for the Friday night service and chanted a few songs to greet the Shabbat.

I then recited the kiddush on some matzah, after first ritually washing my hands. The porters had not yet collected the water basins, which made my life easier. One is not permitted to pour water directly on the ground on Shabbat because this would be part of a prohibition against planting. I was happy that I could pour the water over my hands and back into the wash basin.

The matzah pieces I had varied in size, from small to crumbs. I initially left for Africa with a fresh box, but by the time it had journeyed up a mountain on someone's head, it was not in its original state. In addition to matzah, I had a small sachet of tuna, which completed my Shabbat meal.

"Ben, you coming to dinner?" It was Lance, rounding us up.

"Sure," I said. "I'll be there in a moment."

We gathered in a big tent where a table and chairs were set up. The cook had been instructed about my eating issues, and placed a nice plate of fruit in front of me with a big smile.

"Thanks," I said. On Sunday, I'd instruct him on how to prepare kosher food. Fruit was good, but would not be enough to fuel my body to climb to almost 6,000 meters.

It was our first time sitting down as a group in a relaxed manner. Even though we had met each other before arriving at the mountain, and socialized at the hotel the night before, there is something special about sitting down to your first dinner on the mountain as a unified group. Everyone is more relaxed. There is no rushing to buy or pack some last-minute item. No phone or internet signal is available to cause distraction. And also, after a long day of physical exertion, people tend to drop their barriers. As the masks fall away, the real person emerges.

During the meal, one of the porters brought us large containers of water, which we could use for drinking and to fill our water bottles before going back to our tents. I knew about this procedure, having read about it from someone else's Kilimanjaro climb. Right before Shabbat, I had brought my bottles to the mess tent. When we finished eating and chatting, I left the tent, purposely forgetting my water bottles. A few minutes later, our guide brought them to my tent. "Thank you so much," I said.

Sometimes, it's easier to look forgetful than to try and explain to my Swahili-speaking guide why on Shabbat I can't carry a water bottle twenty feet from one tent to the next.

Taken From, 'G-d is in My Backpack' by: Ben Tanny

Introduction

When I was in Scouts, our scoutmaster was fond of saying, "only the best scouts can camp on Shabbat." What he was implying, was simply that you must be experienced in the outdoors in order to establish a campsite for Shabbat, with a proper eruv, cooking, dining, sleeping, and toilet area.

I've been in a multitude of outdoor situations, from luxurious car camping, where I could set up a tent large enough for me to stand inside, to being cramped in a cocoon-shaped shelter, not much larger than my body. I've camped alone on a mountain in the middle of nowhere, and I've camped at events alongside fifty thousand others. Regardless, I've always found it possible to camp over Shabbat when I wanted to. Though I must say, camping in the snow at high altitude over Shabbat is still providing some logistical challenges.

Shabbat camping does take a bit more preparedness and effort but it's actually not that difficult once you get the hang of it. For those who enjoy camping and being in the outdoors, Shabbat can be a rewarding experience when spent in nature with the opportunity to meditate and have an intimate connection with God and other people. Though, I would not recommend that someone who has not been camping much try it over Shabbat. Camping in general provides enough initial challenges and there's really no need to add to those. Some of my most rewarding experiences and time spent in the outdoors, be it on a canoe trip down a river, hiking though rainforests or climbing a mountain, have been over Shabbat.

Spending time in the outdoors can give you the opportunity to discover and experience more of the beautiful world that G-d has created. The Talmud, Shabbat 77b, displays the wisdom of G-d:

'In all that G-d created in this world, the Holy One did not create a single thing without purpose: thus the snail is a remedy for the scab, the fly is an antidote for the hornet's sting, the mosquito (crushed up) for a snake bite, the snake can cure certain types of boils, and the spider is a remedy for a scorpion (sting).'

G-d is truly everywhere, as are His amazing works. He is no more present in the beauty and purity of nature than in the middle of rush hour traffic amidst a ten-thousand-car traffic jam. G-d is the same, but we are different: most people will probably find it easier to feel His presence and appreciate His creations caught in the former rather than the latter.

If you are new to keeping Shabbat and would like more information in understanding what the source of it is and how we determine what is prohibited, please see the back of the book 'The Essence of Shabbat,' for a quick overview.

I decided to put together this guide because I received many questions via the website www.travelingrabbi.com from people asking for more information about camping on Shabbat. I hope, please G-d, that what is written here will answer a lot of the questions you may have.

Chapter 1: Should You Camp On Shabbat?

Many people may tell you it is not the right thing to do: "It is hard enough to keep Shabbat properly, why put oneself in a position where it will be even more challenging?"

In a way they are right. It is not proper for a Jew to put him or herself in a situation where they will need to compromise on their Judaism. However, I do not see going camping as doing such, provided one works within a Halachic framework of what is and is not permissible.

Those who will tell you not to go camping on Shabbat will largely be people who probably a) don't camp in the first place, b) may not understand your appreciation for camping, and/or c) likely do not have a good understanding of what it means to be camping and how it will affect one's Shabbat.

There are, nonetheless, valid Halachic questions that arise with regards to camping on Shabbat; but so too there are issues with staying at home. Keeping Shabbat in a modern home is actually fairly complicated to the newly observant person. It may seem easy to some of you reading, only because you have grown up doing it or have spent a while getting accustomed to it.

In a modern home you may need to: switch off the light in the fridge, set some lights on timers, put a blech[1] on the stove, fill the hot water urn and plug it in, set a special Shabbat alarm to wake up in the

---

1 'Blech' is Yiddish for 'tin.' It is a flat metallic cover that goes over a burner to permit food to sit on a stove over Shabbat. This only works provided the fire was lit before Shabbat and the food was placed on the blech. The blech serves as a reminder not to adjust the fire.

morning, make sure the outside lights with motion sensor are off, pre-tear toilet paper, and so on.

If you have been keeping Shabbat for years, much of this will be automatic, yet still if you are like most, you will occasionally forget something or accidently switch on a light on Shabbat out of habit.

But as I just mentioned, there are still valid Halachic questions that arise with regards to camping on Shabbat; and the question remains, "Should you put yourself in such a position?"

The way I look at it, there are various types of challenges when it comes to Halachic observance: the first is a personal challenge, which, of course, for every person, is different. When we walk down a street past many seemingly enticing non-kosher restaurants, we may or may not have a strong desire to eat in one of them. For someone who struggles with keeping kosher, it would be better for him or her not to walk down such a street. For others who have been religiously observant their whole lives and for whom the thought of eating non-kosher food may never cross their mind, it is probably fine for them to walk down that street.

The next form of challenge is subject to our current personal circumstances. To the busy businessman, finding time during the day to stop and daven Mincha can be a struggle, whereas for others with a flexible work schedule, it may be easy. Both individuals are determined to make the time to pray, but one is challenged and one is not.

Another form of Halachic challenge occurs when we need to deal creatively with a given situation. For me, I know I want to keep Shabbat and enjoy figuring out how, for example, I can set my tent up so that I will not need to use a flashlight on Friday night. Of course it would be easier for me to just switch a light on and off as needed; but it's not about 'should or should I not turn the light on?' - it is about getting organized and finding creative ways to keep Shabbat when a challenge arises.

If you want to have an easy Jewish life, live in a super-Orthodox community where you can buy all your food at a kosher megastore, where there is a fantastic eruv, and a Synagogue on every corner. If you live in one of these places, you could get by knowing very little Halacha. This is perhaps a good place for some people to be if they struggle with personal observance challenges. Or perhaps even if they don't, they may just enjoy living in a vibrant Jewish community, which is fine.

For me, in the mountains or anywhere in the outdoors, Halacha is a critical aspect. Take, for example, all the laws about how far one must travel to get water for washing hands before eating bread. In normal city life, this does not usually apply very often. You find a tap and turn it on. But hiking through the desert or in a mountain area, this may very well be a real situation. The challenge for me is not whether or not I should wash my hands; rather, it is, *how* will I wash my hands within an acceptable Halachic framework?"

When there is no kosher megastore, you need to know the laws of kosher very well to figure out what is or is not kosher to eat. And when there are no synagogues, you need to know how to pray, where to pray, and when to pray. I don't mean to suggest to anyone to pack up and go camping in a remote mountainous area - because if you don't like camping, you'll dislike it even more if you try it over

Shabbat, or even during the week while having to deal with Halachic issues. If you enjoy camping, and a bit of adventure, then I believe G-d wants you to go camping and still stay strong with Halacha.

Judaism is about living our lives in our real world, each one of us, whatever this may be. The Torah recognized that some people would be camel drivers, some sailors, and some businessmen; and each would need their own Halachic parameters within which to work. So these parameters have been provided for us.

Why not become vegetarian, and have only a dairy kitchen? You'd never need to worry about mixing up dishes or anything to do with cooking meat and milk together. Shechita (ritual slaughter), koshering the meat through salting and removing the forbidden parts of the animal, are highly complex areas in which it can take years to become proficient and knowledgeable. It would be easier to do away with the whole thing, and some people do. There are perhaps a half a billion vegetarian Hindus, so obviously living without consuming meat is possible. But the Torah realizes that many of us would like to eat meat and gives us a way to do it and a code of Jewish law for dealing with problems as they come up.

So if you like camping, go camping on Shabbat as well. Just make sure to do it within the proper Halachic framework.

Chapter 2: Be Prepared

The foundation of my camping knowledge was gained in my first year of scouting. The Boy Scout motto is 'Be Prepared'; and certainly when it came to heading out to camp over Shabbat, it is essential that we are ready for the extra challenges that Shabbat will bring.

If you are planning on camping, you need to be prepared. Most problems arise from being unprepared, and this is undoubtedly the case when it comes to camping over Shabbat.

> *A group of us scouts once went on a week-long canoe trip. Before heading out, my canoeing/tenting partner and I selected a troop tent, set it up, and checked that it was in good order, with all parts working. After our first long day of canoeing, we arrived on an island where we set up camp. When we tried putting up our tent, we discovered that the two clamps for holding the A-frame tent together were missing. This meant it was impossible to keep the tent standing. After checking into the situation, we discovered that two scouts in the group had not checked their troop tent before loading them for the trip, and ours had gotten mixed up with theirs in the car as the bags both looked the same.*

I cannot express enough how important it is to make sure everything is in order. You think your flashlight/headlamp is going to work because you replaced the batteries a week ago? Unknown to you, looking for batteries to run his toy, your kid took the batteries out of your flashlight; and now you have a non-functioning light. Or you have a nice eruv building kit which you used last summer, but you've forgotten that when you needed nails for building your sukkah, you took them from the eruv kit. Now you arrive at your campsite, it's a half hour to Shabbat (you left early but got stuck in traffic) and you have no nails and no way to set up the eruv.

Check everything, and don't just assume things will be in order when you arrive at your campsite.

Make sure you have enough time on Friday afternoon after arriving at your campsite to set up properly. I've seen it happen many times; people get to the campsite late on a Friday afternoon and do not have the required time to set up. Having ample time will certainly make things easier and more relaxed. Just think of the pre-Shabbat chaos that goes on in a religious home on a Friday late afternoon and multiply that if you are in the outdoors where you are in the blazing sun, flies are annoying you and mosquitoes biting you.

On Friday afternoon, along with setting up for Shabbat itself, it's also great to get things in order for motzei Shabbat. What are you planning to do when Shabbat ends? Perhaps you want to have a bonfire, cook dinner or conduct an activity? Now, if you are camping in the summer (which is highly probable) Shabbat may end at nine or ten o'clock. At this time you don't want to be gathering wood, getting a BBQ to work, or emptying the car in search of your havdala[2] kit. Thus, your Friday preparation for Shabbat should also leave enough time to prepare for after Shabbat.

2A ceremony marking the end of Shabbat, marking a separation between the holiness of Shabbat and the rest of the week. It consist of a prayer over wine, smelling spices, and a blessing over fire.

A good person to have along with you on a Shabbat camping trip is a non-Jew. For a period of time, I was part of a Jewish Scout troop where a non-Jew had joined for whatever reason. He was happy to be the 'Shabbos goy,' as he called himself, and he knew what to do without being told. Because he was part of the troop, anything he did was for himself and did not prove to be a Halachic problem. If a gas lantern went out in the eating area, he'd re-light it. So having a non Jewish friend or companion along with you could be handy, though not always practical.

If you are camping in a public campground, you could make friends with the non-Jewish people camped next to you. Talk to them about Shabbat on Friday afternoon already. Asking a non-Jew to do things on Shabbat can be problematic, but educating them prior to Shabbat to understand what you may need help with Halachically can work better. This way they may just do something automatically; or when you need help with something, they will get the hint.

There are a few key areas that need preparation for, which we will look at briefly here and then later on in more detail.

Sleeping Facilities: If you are sleeping in a tent, it must be correctly set up a good spot. Keep in mind that it is forbidden to tie knots or drive stakes into the ground on Shabbat, which means if your tent blows over in a strong wind or begins to leak during a downpour you may not be able to adjust the lines and the stakes connecting the tent. It is not uncommon for beginner campers to realize in the middle of the night that they have pitched their tent in a bad spot. The area may not drain water properly, or the tent could be sitting in a wind tunnel.

Don't be lazy. Be a perfectionist and make sure every stake is in properly, the rain cover is tied strongly, and all knots are secure.

It is Halachically permissible to put the rainfly on to an already erected tent, or remove it, provided no knots are tied or stakes driven into the ground.

If you are sleeping in a vehicle/station wagon/RV camper, have you disconnected the lights? When you open the doors are any lights going to turn on? Are you sleeping in the back of a station wagon and the vehicle only has electric windows? Have you put them down? What if it rains and you can't put them back up?

Do you have a light source in your tent which you will be leaving on? If not, then it is important to have everything organized inside the tent, like your pyjamas already laid out, tissues if you will need to blow your nose, and perhaps a warm hat in which to sleep if the weather is cold. You basically should be able to find everything you will need with your eyes closed.

Eating area: Where do you plan on eating over Shabbat? Will you be sitting at a picnic table, on the ground, or in your tent? Do you have enough water to use for food preparation, washing and drinking? How about purifying water? If you are using a battery operated water purifier, have you prepared enough? Where will your dirty dishes go if you cannot wash them on Shabbat? Is it safe to leave them out or will animals come, attracted by the leftovers?

Food: What do you plan on eating? Do you have any sort of refrigeration with you or perhaps an ice box that can keep food cool?

Do you intend on eating cooked food on Shabbat day that you might need to prepare on Friday? Do you have challah or matzah or do you plan on baking some sort of bread? Where are you leaving the food, in a car, tent, container or bear bag? and can it be accessed and moved on Shabbat?

Toilet Facilities: Where will you go to the toilet? Are you using a public toilet and is there toilet paper already there for you to use? Can this paper be used on Shabbat? Will you be leaving paper in the toilet area for your personal use if you cannot carry it on Shabbat?

For backcountry camping, where do you plan on going? You will need to dig a hole before Shabbat and prepare some leaves, branches or paper etc. If you wake in the middle of the night and it's pitch black, will you be able to find the toilet area?

Urinating on the ground is not a problem with regards to watering plants, because the caustic fluid doesn't help the plant. However, there is an opinion that holds urine is beneficial to plants. When possible, it is good to urinate on a rock if you want to be extra strict. There are some questions regarding urinating over dirt because this could be part of a melacha[3] that relates to forming mud, but it is probably not any major concern to the camper.

Eruv: Carrying items from one domain to another, or even within one area that is open, is prohibited on Shabbat. An eruv is a form of an enclosure that permits objects to be moved around within the

---

3 There are 39 categories of activities known as 'avmelachot' forbidden to be done on Shabbat. Everything prohibited on Shabbat relates to these core 39 . See 'Essence of Shabbat,' at the end of book, for more information.

confines of the area. Do you intend on building an eruv or will you organize everything so that you will not need to carry things around from one place to another?

Tip:Some people have a checklist which they use at home before Shabbat. The idea behind the list is to remind them of everything that needs to get done before Shabbat. Everyone's list is different. One person's list may have "Switch off fridge light," whereas someone else may have a fridge with a Sabbath mode that does this automatically. Or, they may choose to leave the light off all the time.

It is a good idea to create your own personal pre-Shabbat Camping checklist and list everything that relates to your personal camping style.

Chapter 3: Camping Styles

Three Styles of Camping

There are three principal styles of camping which will affect one's ability to keep Shabbat:

1. *Car camping:* This is where you are going to drive to a campsite and park where you intend to camp. Weight is not an issue as you can bring as many things as you need. This style involves the fewest obstacles because it's possible to carry building materials for an eruv, extra water to wash for bread, and additional cooking utensils, along with lights, candles etc.

2. *Backcountry camping:* This is where you will be carrying everything with you to the campsite. You could use a backpack, canoe, or even a bicycle to transport your food and gear. You will probably need to be mindful of how much weight you are transporting, though you can usually bring a bit extra, since it is for a short period only. For example, you are hiking in on a Friday afternoon to your campsite, but it's only a half an hour's walk or so, and thus you are able to carry more than you would if you were on a multi-day trip. Or even if you've left on a Thursday, but are only going for a few days and therefore won't be carrying food to last a week or two.

3. *Extreme backcountry camping:* This is where every ounce of weight counts and you have no space to carry anything extra. You may be on an extended week, two weeks, or a month long trip along a wilderness track. This method of camping is by far the most challenging because it really takes some planning and creativity to figure out exactly what you will need to keep Shabbat. If you are traveling in this style, hopefully you are an experienced hiker/camper. This means that you should have the knowhow and creativity to come up with and apply solutions to assist with keeping Shabbat. For example: you may not want to build an eruv, however you should have the organizational skills to set your campsite up well enough that nothing needs to be moved. You'll probably also be able to set up your tent for Shabbat so that you can find everything without light.

If you are new to camping or new to keeping Shabbat, I would not recommend trying anything over Shabbat beyond car camping, until you have done it two to three times and are comfortable with it.

One of the biggest challenges for newbies in camping or keeping Shabbat is habits. We all have them. It's what we do automatically without thinking. Thus, for the newly initiated Shabbat observer, it is important to put something over the light switches at home so they don't absentmindedly flick a switch. For people who have grown up their entire life observant they may not need to do this.

The same applies to many aspects of camping. If you are new to sitting on the ground, it's easy to pick up a rock or stick and begin to play with it. This is prohibited on Shabbat. An experienced camper may hang his or her hat on a tree without thinking, which is also a problem on Shabbat. Therefore it is important to make life in the campsite as easy as possible from the outset, so that campers can stay aware of what they are doing.

Packing a Torah

If you are camping with a group and will have a minayn, you could take a Torah with you. With car camping, size and weight may not matter, though smaller is better because it will take up less space.

It is possible to take a Torah on a backpacking trip, though you'd probably want a small one. You can see a video of a beautiful sefer Torah around 5 inches high:http://tinyurl.com/pg9fd8k. This would easily fit in a backpack.

On a less extreme level, Torahs one to one and a half feet in length are more common and can still be taken in a backpack if you are super keen. The important thing is to keep the Torah protected from the elements during transportation and reading. For car camping, wrap the Torah in a tallit and place it in a plastic container, such as the ones sold in Walmart/Kmart, and similar type stores. This will keep it safe. For backpacking, place the Torah in dry bags and then a plastic container. It is important that, any container or bag used be designated specifically for the Torah and treated with respect.

When you read the Torah, make sure the area is completely dry and that there is no chance of it getting wet.

I have travelled with tefillin[4] in my backpack through extreme environments over mountains, through jungles and across deserts. I've fallen into a river with my backpack on. Thank G-d, my tefillin have always stayed safe in their waterproof container. So it is possible to backpack with a Torah.

4Tefillinare a set of small black leather boxes containing scrolls of parchment inscribed with verses from the Torah, which are worn by men during weekday morning prayers.

Camping on Shabbat

Chapter 4: When to Start and Finish Shabbat

Shabbat Start and Finishing Times

You can find out what time Shabbat starts and finishes anywhere in the world. Go to Google Maps and zoom in on the area where you will be camping. Right click on the spot and you will be given an option, 'What's Here?' Click on this and you will get the longitude and latitude of the area, which will look something like this: -35.535579,138.44556

Next, go to www.myzmanim.com and insert the numbers. You should get all the times you need.

If you're unable to determine the start and finishing time of Shabbat, it's best to be more stringent and bring in Shabbat a bit earlier and end it a bit later than what it might be, giving an extra ten minutes on both ends. If you are able to see the sun set clearly over an ocean, lake, or field, you can tell when Shabbat is going to start, but in the mountains or forest, this won't work. Shabbat ends when three stars are visible. If it's clouded over then this is not always practical.

Keep in mind that because it may be dark, you might not be able to see the time on a clock or watch. An option is to set an alarm on your phone or watch to indicate when Shabbat is over.

Bringing Shabbat in Early

Generally I find this very practical when camping in the summer as Shabbat comes in late. I find it easier to bring Shabbat in an hour early. This way I can daven, eat, and clean up before it gets dark. It makes life a lot simpler than trying to do stuff in the dark. Of course, if you have a proper light source set up then this won't be an issue.

The earliest it is permissible to bring Shabbat in early, light candles, daven maariv[5], and recite Kiddush is from 'plaghamincha,' which is 1 ¼ 'Halachic hours' before sunset. In Jewish time, the day and night are both divided into 12 Halachic hours, no matter how many 'real' hours they each last. So in the summer when there is more daylight, a Halachic hour will be longer than 60 minutes. And in the winter, a daytime hour could be less than 60 minutes. Check www.myzmanim.com to find out what time plaghamincha will be in your camping area. If you have mobile phone reception where you are camping, you can also use the Pocket Luach Deluxe app (or a similar app), which calculates the exact times based on your coordinates.

5Maariv is also known as Arvit. It is the third prayer session of the day followed by Shacharit in the morning, Mincha in the afternoon, and then Maariv which is usually recited after nightfall.

Chapter 5: Bathing and Clean Clothes

Bathing

In honor of Shabbat it's important to wash oneself on Friday afternoon. If you have showers at your campground, you could use them. Perhaps there is a lake where you can go for a swim, or a small river in which to rinse off. However, the mitzvah of washing before Shabbat is best done with warm water. In a situation where it's very cold and you have no desire to enter freezing water, or there is little water available, for the sake of the honor of Shabbat you should at least wash your hands, face and feet with warm water. In situations where you may be snow camping and do not want to wash your feet due to a risk of frostbite, I think it's fine to skip the feet washing. Dirty feet were common when people wore open shoes along dusty or dirty roads. Chances are, if you have been hiking for any period of time, your socks and boots will smell so bad that washing your feet won't make a difference. Though certainly if you can, then you should.

If you are car camping, you could get a solar shower. This is a large bag which you fill with water in the morning and hang it from a tree. The sun heats it up, and in the afternoon you can have a hot shower. They work reasonably well.

A nice way to wash off when hot water is scarce is to heat a small pot of water, wet a wash cloth and wipe your body down.

Tip: If you are using a paid campground, the showers may be coin operated. Keep this in mind if you are used to taking a last minute pre Shabbat shower. You'll want to make sure you have change ready because if it takes you ten minutes to find coins it could mean no time to shower if you are running late.

Clothing

Wearing special clothing for Shabbat is important. There is much written about this in the Talmud; stories of great sages and their special Shabbat garments. We know about Tzadikim who donned special clothing just for Shabbat, and immediately after Shabbat changed out of them to retain their uniqueness. It's important for us to keep this in mind when we are camping, because too often it's easy to just say 'These are my camping clothes, and I'll just wear them for Shabbat as well.'

If you are camping on a regular basis, then perhaps try to bring special camping clothing for Shabbat. Obviously you don't want to have a designer dress or suit, fancy pants or shiny polished shoes. The suit, tie, and black hat won't fare well either in a rough outdoor environment. You want practical clothing that functions well in the outdoors. Find something that works and is special for Shabbat. If this is not possible, then at the minimum try to wear clean clothes for Shabbat. If you have no clean clothes, put on the cleanest of your dirty clothing!

With extreme backcountry camping, where it's not practical to carry anything extra, what I've done at times is to at least have a special kippah . This doesn't weigh anything.

I was once a counsellor on a program where we took teenagers on a one-month hike across Israel. During the trip, we spent three Shabbatot in the outdoors where we camped. Everyone had a special white shirt for Shabbat; and even though after one week in the backpack it was no longer white, it was still special.

Chapter 6: Shabbat Candles and Campsite Lighting

Shabbat Candles

The challenge with lighting Shabbat candles while camping is the high probability of a wind coming and blowing them out. You may also be in a situation where local law does not permit lighting any fire. This is common in places like Australia where there can be a total fire ban. I've experimented with several kinds of candleholders sold in camping shops, designed to hold tea light candles. Some of them hold a special size of larger candles. These holders are usually made from metal and glass containers that you can hang. I've met with different degrees of success but have not found any of them to be perfect. When it's windy, the candles seem at some point to get blown out one way or the other, regardless of how well they have been placed. There are some larger lantern-type holders that work well, though they are bulky and heavy and can only be brought if you are car camping.

There is a dispute amongst the Halachic authorities, dating back to when electricity first came into use, as to whether electric lights can satisfy our obligation to light Shabbat candles. Electric lights, like candles, satisfy the two reasons given for lighting Shabbat candles in the first place: 1) Shalom Bayit, which means 'Peace in the home.' A house without lights isn't harmonious if its occupants are crashing into each other; and 2) Oneg Shabbat, which means 'joy of

Shabbat.' A nicely lit home will bring more joy to the Shabbat, as people can see each other and what they are eating.

There are many authorities who even allow a beracha (blessing) to be said on electric lights for Shabbos, while according to others you may light it in honor of Shabbat but not make a beracha on such a lighting.

Rav Shlomo ZalmanAuerbachztz"l, a very esteemed Halachic authority, differentiated between an electric lamp that is connected to an electrical power socket, and a battery-powered light. Rabbi Auerbach held that the battery is like the oil or the fuel of the candle and it is permissible to make a beracha on it, but not on a light connected to a main power plant.

It may be fine to rely on this in emergency situations when it is not possible to light with an open flame, such as in hotels, hospitals, and in our case when camping. As with anything else in this book, be sure to ask your local rabbi.

Campsite Lighting

If you are in a dark area, it's good to tie a few glow sticks (also known as snap lights) around the site. Tie one to each tent, one by your eating area and one by the toilet. Consider whether if someone needs to use the bathroom in middle of the night they will be able to find their way to and from it or not.

Glow sticks can usually be found in a dollar shop or similar type store, and if not, are easily available on Amazon and eBay. There are some very bright glow sticks you can get which last around 12 hours, and when hung in a tent will give plenty of light. They are fairly cheap and should cost anywhere from $0.25-$1/piece

Nowadays virtually all portable hand held lights are made with LED. A small flashlight or head lamp could easily burn for 100 hours on a set of new batteries. It's simple just to hang a couple of small head lamps around your camping area and one in your tent. Just have some extra batteries to use after Shabbat and you should be fine. The nice thing about an LED light in the tent is that you can have light to read and see what is going on; and when you want to sleep, there is no safety issue of covering it with an item of clothing, as there would be with another type of light.

There are 'solar powered walkway lights' that can work well. People often use them on their walkways leading to their home. They are super lightweight, drive into the ground easily and have a small solar panel on the top. You could get a bunch of these to put around the campsite. They should cost around $3/unit with a set of ten usually around $30.

Chapter 7: Food Preparation

Food Preparation and Cooking

It is forbidden to cook food on Shabbat, and therefore all food will need to be prepared beforehand. Having hot food on Shabbat day is nice and adds to the OnegShabat, but is not practical in a camping context unless you have some sort of electric source, for example if you are camping in a powered site. If this is the case, you could plug in a slow cooker and have a cholent[6], or plug in a hot plate to heat food.

Friday night there are few more options for hot food. One is to finish cooking the food right before Shabbat. Depending on what time Shabbat comes in and how long it will be before eating, you can take the food, wrap it in towels (make sure it's not going to leak) and put it inside a sleeping bag. Then cover it with additional sleeping bags if you have. Things like potatoes, eggs or even soup could stay warm like this for a couple of hours. It is important to note that using this method to keep food hot is only permitted in the case where the materials used for wrapping the food will not heat the food up further. If one wrapped food in hot coals, an electric blanket etc., it is forbidden to use the food on Shabbat.

Another method is, if you are using any sort of camping stove, you can insert a small gas cylinder that will run out after a short

---

6A traditional Jewish stew eaten for lunch on Shabbat. It is set to cook from before Shabbat and thereby is permitted to be eaten on Shabbat. Sephardim have a similar dish called 'hamim.'

period of time. There is a common type sold in Walmart/Kmart for around $20 that comes with 4 gas cylinders (you can purchase additional cylinders). You just leave one in and let it burn itself out. You probably don't want to hook up a stove to a big propane gas tank unless you don't mind burning it out.

While we are on the topics of lighting and cooking, you may be thinking "why not set up a bonfire right before Shabbat?" The key problem with this, I believe, is that there is a tendency to throw things into a bonfire without thinking. People sit around the fire and casually throw in a twig, leaf etc. This is prohibited. That's why when cooking on stove, we use a blech (a metallic plate) to cover over the flame, in order to remind us not to adjust the heat.

The rabbis were always concerned that someone would manipulate a fire source on Shabbat to get more light or heat without thinking. For this reason it is forbidden to read next to an oil lamp because one may tilt it to make the oil run more, so as to better see what one is reading. Perhaps if you had a gate around the bonfire it could serve a reminder, though this really is not practical. So I suggest setting up a bonfire area and saving it for Saturday night.

Cooked Food for Shabbat Day

In cold temperatures, it is not much of an issue to prevent your food from going off. But when camped out in hot weather, you may find that by Shabbat midday the cooked food from Friday is starting to taste a bit funny. Food usually keeps longer in as plain a form as possible, so if you cook rice or pasta, don't mix it up with any sauce or it will go off sooner. Keep the sauce separate and only add it when you are ready to eat. Don't eat any cooked animal products on Shabbat day if you have no refrigeration. If you'd like to have meat, bring a frozen salami and keep it on ice, it should still be fine for Shabbat day. For fish: canned fish is good, but opening the can is a problem (creating a vessel on Shabbat) and you won't want to leave an open can of fish in your campsite from Friday evening. A good option if you can find kosher ones in your area is tuna sachets. This is tuna with the liquid already drained and packed tightly in a foil sachet. Some companies make already seasoned in the package types which are fantastic for Shabbat camping and camping in general.

I use hard-boiled eggs for up to 24 hours out of the fridge if they are kept in cool temperatures. Hard cheese is usually fine for a few days out of a fridge.

Putting the food in Ziploc bags is great. Keep the food in the shade. If you have some cold water, float the bags in the water; this will keep it cool. If weight is not an issue then bring an esky/cooler. No ice, just fill a few empty plastic soda bottles with water and freeze them before you head out. This will keep things cool and provide you with water which you will probably need anyway.

Cooking for Shabbat and Recipes

On Shabbat, it is important to eat well, and when camping there is no reason to compromise. On my own I won't bother with anything fancy, mostly because I haven't the patience, though I've been on Shabbat camp outs where participants spent all Friday afternoon cooking up a feast. If you think it's not possible to prepare incredible food while camping in the outdoors, there are climbing groups who specifically climb to the top of a mountain and set up a fancy dinner, with tables, chairs and multiple food courses. These people are passionate about both food and climbing. So if you love the outdoors and you love your cooking, then take the challenge and learn how to make incredible food in the outdoors. Camp cooking and baking is a skill, and for many, it is part of the fun of camping. If you are heading out on Friday you could bring all your food readymade, or you might enjoy the challenge of learning to cook over a camp fire, with a Dutch oven, foil cooking, or BBQ.

One secret to making tasty camping food without carrying large amounts of spices and ingredients is to use fresh garlic and onion. It's amazing what a little bit of fresh onion or garlic can do to a package of instant rice or noodles.

Important note: In the likely event that a kamikaze bug lands in your food, it is important to be careful how you remove the bug. Separating items on Shabbat can be a Halachic problem. Remove the bug along with some food and it is okay.

Bear Bags

A bear bag is a term used for setting up a system where a bag of food is hung between two trees. Most of the time, leaving food on the ground will attract anything from large animals like bears and wild boars, to small pesky animals like raccoons, chipmunks, and mice. In bear country, setting up a proper system is critical. In areas where there are no bears it may still be important because of other animals, however the height and distance from the tree trunk is not as important to get right. If you are unfamiliar with setting up a bear bag, Google it and you'll find plenty of information.

With regards to Shabbat, it is forbidden to hang anything or touch anything that is directly connected to a living or dead tree, for fear of breaking a branch. For this reason, lying in hammock connected directly to a tree may also be a problem. This said, it is possible to set things up to be used on Shabbat. The object needs to be connected to a peg attached to the tree. This is called 'tzdadindi'tzdadin' (sides of the sides). This does not need to be a peg, per se; it can be a chain, a rope or something else. So when setting up a bear bag, you create a loop of rope to go around a branch and then thread your main rope through the loop. In this way, you are using the tree indirectly. The same applies for a hammock.

Chapter 8: How to Bake Bread in the Outdoors

There are various methods for baking bread on a camping trip; in a frying pan, Dutch oven or pot, or even in a pile of ashes like the Bedouins do. You can make many styles of flat bread like Indian chappatis, or steamed bread in a can, or if you like, try some Mexican Sopapillas. People made bread in the outdoors long before we had modern kitchens and there are many ways to do it.

For example, on a week-long camel trip in Rajasthan India, twice a day our guide baked chappatis on a metal plate over a small fire. It only took him about 10-20 minutes, depending on how many were being made.

When I worked as a counsellor for Jewish outdoor trips that included Shabbat, we usually made fried bread in a pan, as this is a fairly simple and failproof method for first timers.

Learning to cook or bake bread in the outdoors can be a fun activity to do, by yourself, with family or with friends. Yet keep in mind, late on Friday afternoon is not the time that you want to start experimenting and trying to make a new type of bread for the first time. You may want to practice before you head out to camp, like on a Sunday afternoon; or perhaps on a Friday in your home kitchen/backyard - that way, if the bread turns out, you can use it for Shabbat. You might also want to take a box of matzah with you on your camping trip, which will alleviate stress from any Friday afternoon baking failure.

Fry It

Almost any dough can be fried. Follow a recipe for basic bread and let the dough rise. Then, instead of forming loaves, roll or pat the dough on a solid surface until it is roughly ½-inch thick. Next, slice the dough into wedges and separate the pieces. Wait for it to rise again until the pieces are twice as thick. Then, heat a pan of oil on a camping stove or over a fire and wait until the oil is hot. Slip the pieces of dough a few at a time, depending on the size of your pan. When one side is browned, turn the piece over and fry the other side. Place the bread on paper towels when done, or on something where the excess oil can drain off.

Boil It

Traditional bagels are boiled! Well, first boiled and then baked. To make boiled bread, follow a basic dough recipe and form the dough into a circular bagel shapes. Let them rise. Next, gently slip the pieces into a large pan of rapidly boiling water. Using a slotted spoon, remove the bread when it is firm. Let the bread dry, and then fry lightly on each side in a lightly greased skillet. This will finish the cooking and give them a nice crisp outside. The boiling method has the advantage of using far less oil. This could work well in backcountry camping where you don't want to carry much weight.

Bake It

You can bake bread even without an oven. It's simple to do on most outdoor grills. For baking to work properly, you need heat from both above and below. If your grill has a cover then you can close it to create an oven-like environment. If there is no cover, try using a bucket or metal mixing bowl over the bread. This will capture the heat and direct it downwards, back onto the bread. You may also need to raise the bread so that it is not too close to the heat. Use some empty tuna cans, a pan or anything else to elevate the bread; but pay attention that what you use does not insulate the bread from the heat. Baking should take anywhere from 15-30 minutes, depending on the size.

Dutch oven: These are heavy cast iron things that will only work with car camping. You won't want to carry one more than a hundred feet. I've cooked (and burnt!) all kinds of foods in these. Getting the temperature and timing right is important. The upside is, you can bake a traditional challah if you choose. To make bread, line the Dutch oven with aluminium foil. Place the dough directly on the foil, or, alternatively, make a loaf of bread in a pan, placing the pan in the oven with the bread in it. Put the oven into a pile of coals and cover the top with more coals. Check online to learn more about Dutch oven baking.

With pans: Using two pans one on top of the other, forming a makeshift oven, you can bake bread between them. Remember to cover the top pan with hot coals, as you are trying to get as much heat from above as below.

Steam It

Steamed breads are very common around the world, in places where people do not have ovens. There are many ways to do this. In camping situations, you can use an empty tin can covered with a lid or foil. You'll need a trivet - real or makeshift - so that the can/pan/pot does not sit directly on the heat source. If you are in a powered campsite, you could bring a slow cooker and steam the bread in it. Research more online if this method of baking interests you.

Flatten It

There are many styles of flat bread. Flat bread can be made over a fire, over a heated rock or in an oven. Matzah is a form of flat bread. You basically mix flour and water, knead it for a few minutes, roll the dough into balls, flatten it and cook for a minute or so.

Chapter 9: Going to the Toilet and Washing Hands

Toilet Area

When camping in the wild, you will need to prepare a latrine lavatory area before Shabbat. It should be far enough from your camp site that it does not contaminate the area, though it should be easily accessible without the need of a flashlight, should you need it in the dark.

Dig an appropriate number of holes, depending on how many people you are. Leave a pile of dirt next to the hole along with a trowel so that the dirt can be pushed into the hole. If you are using paper, leave some in a Ziploc bag weighted down by a rock. Rocks and branches are considered 'muktzah,' [7] unless they are set aside from before Shabbat for a specific purpose. In this case you have set it aside to use as a paperweight, so it is okay. Similarly, if you plan on using rocks or branches to wipe with, select and prepare them next to the hole before Shabbat.

You may also want to tie a glow stick or two near the area to make it findable in the dark. If you see that the area will be a bit challenging to reach in the dark, you could string a line from your

---

[7] On Shabbat one avoids handling objects associated with weekday activities, or whose handling may result in a Shabbat violation. There are two general categories of muktzah 1) Strictmuktzah and 2) light muktzeh. In general, items that are never used on Shabbat are considered strict muktzah, while items that are sometimes used are considered light muktzah. A rock that could serve a purpose, for example as a paperweight for toilet paper, would come under the classification as 'light muktzah.'

campsite before Shabbat. This way, in the dark, people can hold the string and follow it to and from the toilet area.

In the case that you have to go and no area was prepared before Shabbat, try and find a spot that the excrement can fall to, like between some rocks. You should not dig a hole on Shabbat. Once done you should cover it a bit if possible by kicking some sand or rocks over it. After Shabbat return and cover it properly.

If you are car camping somewhere with no bathroom facilities, you can make a toilet that will work well on Shabbat and in general. Get a plastic (usually white) 20Lt/5Gal bucket. Place two garbage bags inside and a toilet seat on the top and you've got a good camp toilet that eliminates any Shabbat toilet issues. When you leave the camp site, you can tie the bags shut and then secure the plastic lid on the bucket. This should transport well until you find somewhere to dispose the waste.

Washing Hands

You will want to wash your hands in the morning after waking up or at some point after going to the toilet. You may also want to wash your hands before eating bread. What's important to keep in mind is that it's forbidden to pour water directly onto the ground because this would be considered to be one aspect of the work of planting, a forbidden activity.

However, it is permissible to pour water over rocks or some other surface, even if the water will then slide onto vegetation - so long as it does not fall directly onto the vegetation. If there is no large rock in the area, gather a few rocks in a pile before Shabbat, to serve as a washing station over which you can pour water.

Chapter 10: Building an Eruv

Building an eruv comes with many complications. If I am camping alone or with just another person or two I find it easier to set up the campsite in such a way that we don't actually need an eruv. It is permissible to carry something up to 6 feet within a non-enclosed area. This means if you are sitting on a chair you can move it a little if you need to, or any other non-muktzah object. For example, if I know I will want to lie on the grass on Shabbat afternoon and read a book, I put the book inside a plastic Ziploc bag and leave it outside before Shabbat. This way, I don't have to carry the book from my tent to where I'd like to lie on the grass. If it's a siddur or Torah book, I try and place it on a rock, or log a bit above the ground out of respect.

You can set up your eating area in a spot where you won't need to move things around; or perhaps you have an extra tent that you can set up as a kitchen. Here, though, you must be very careful, and should not use the non-eruv method if there is any chance you might carry.

With a couple of adults or mature teens who won't need to move things about, the above can work. But if you are camping with children or a larger group of people then it becomes more complicated for people to organize themselves, or to serve larger meals. It's almost impossible to ensure that no one is going to carry anything, so in this case putting up in an eruv is undoubtedly the way to go.

To make an eruv you are going to need materials, so it's really only practical if you can carry the extra weight in a car. Sometimes you might be able to camp somewhere where an eruv is not needed because it is sort of partially set up - for example, a completely fenced-in campground, or paddock. Where a camper van has an extendable awning, you are allowed to carry beneath the awning. You might also find some natural features that can serve as part of an eruv. A solid cliff wall or very thick, impenetrable bushes can suffice. A couple of vans parked close together along with a wall of closely set up tents may also serve as an eruv, if set up correctly.

If you're going backcountry camping but only walking a short distance to get to your campsite, you can carry the extra weight of the building materials. For extreme backcountry camping you are limited to what you can carry; however, it is still possible to build an eruv, which will be explained further on.

How to Build an Eruv While Camping

Building an eruv is a fairly complex Halachic endeavour. The Talmudic tractate 'Eruvin' is considered to be one of the most difficult to study. That said, building an eruv can be complicated or simple depending on the situation. Imagine building an eruv in a city versus for a bungalow colony. These will be two very different structures but the Halachot of eruvin would still apply equally for both.

I attended Jewish summer camps where there was always an eruv set up, although younger campers never took part in it, a shame as that would have been a good learning experience. I myself only got really involved when I joined a troop of Shomer Shabbat Boy Scouts at the age of twelve, and we often set up eruvin. It would be hard for me to remember how many we put up over the years, whether around our campsite or an outdoor synagogue. The eruv could be something more permanent or something very temporary. Sometimes we planned to leave it up for a month and sometimes just for the weekend.

My most interesting eruv building experience happened in Israel. I, along with another madrich (leader), led a group of teenagers on a one-month trip along the Israel Trail. Part of the program and educational experience was to teach the boys how to build an eruv.

I'm now going to share some ideas here, but please note that if you are serious about camping on Shabbat and building an eruv, I recommend you find a local rabbi in your community who could study some of the laws with you. It's important to note that not all rabbis are knowledgeable in the laws of eruv.

The Laws of an Eruv

My intention here is not to go into the laws of eruv as to what is a *ReshutHaRabim*(a public domain with regards to Halacha), *ReshutHaYachid*(a private domain with regards to Halacha), a *Karmelit* (a non-enclosed area that does not qualify as a *ReshutHaRabim*). You should find somewhere else to study about this.

What I want here is to look at a practical approach to building an eruv when camping.

One note about eruv that is important to understand: It is permissible to carry in a closed structure, but what do we do if say a wall is missing? Answer: we can create something that stands in for a wall and defines the structure as a closed one. This something is an archway of sorts, known as 'TzuratHaPetach,' and what an eruv creates is generally a series of many archways like these. There is no limit to how many archways there can be. If real walls (house, fence, etc.) are available, that's great; but even if there are no real walls you can keep making archways.

The easiest way to construct a Halachic archway is to connect from one lechi (pole) to another with fishing string.

An important idea to keep in mind is that you may be able to create an actual walled-in space for a small area instead of relying on making a TzuratHaPetach. For example, if you could use a roll of mesh or plastic tarpaulin or the like: you may be able to encircle an area by tying mesh or tarpaulin to some poles, between cars, or even trees. This can sometimes be easier than making an eruv.

A good book to exploreeruvin in more detail is 'The Contemporary Eruv, Revised & Expanded Edition: Eruvin in Modern Metropolitan Areas' by Rabbi Yosef GavrielBechhofer. This book is more geared towards building a city eruv, but many of the principles discussed will apply to building a camping eruv, for example, if and when a cliff face could be used as part of an eruv, etc.

Materials Needed

❖ *'Lechis' (poles):* Look for poles around 4 feet long because you may want to drive them a bit into the ground and you still want them to be higher than ten tefachim[8], which is the minimum. You also don't want to run a line so low that someone will trip on it or a kid will run into it.

❖ If you plan to leave the eruv up for longer than a weekend, get 1 inch × 1 inch slats of wood, or one-inch diameter bamboo, which will hold up better. If space and weight is an issue, then thin pieces of bamboo will do. If you are camping in an open field area, you could get by with four poles by constructing a square around your camp site. When camped in a wooded area it gets trickier because you will need to scoot around trees. For one to two families camping together, I'd take ten poles.

❖ *Nails:* Drive a nail into the top of each pole. Make sure to have additional nails with you as some may fall out. Note that the fishing line must pass directly above the lechi and may not be wrapped around the top of the pole.

❖ *Fishing string:* This is to connect one pole to another. Fishing string is good because it stays taut, which is important. If the eruv line sags too much and moves around in the wind (which could be the case when using nylon rope or twine), the eruv will not be kosher.

---

8 Atefach is a handbreadth in length equalling 3.15 inches, or according to a stricter opinion, 3.78 inches.

❖ *Cord:* Cut a few dozen three-foot-long pieces. Cord should be about the weight of a hiking boot lace. You will need these to connect the poles to rocks, trees, cars, etc.

❖ *An Eruv Bag:* this is what you keep all the eruv supplies in. It will make it easy for you to set up and take down an eruv quickly. It's important to be organized. I've seen it happen often when arriving at a camp site Friday afternoon that there's not much time to set up the tents, cook the food, etc. The last thing you want is to spend half an hour looking for the spare nails.

Extreme Backcountry Camping: If you are at least two people and you have at least four trekking poles, think about how you could use them. You could attach a small upside-down screw to the top with duct tape, and then use some fishing line to wrap around the screw. You should have a pair of extra shoelaces with you, which you can use to secure the poles to trees. This method of eruv building is actually fairly simple, and if you are camped in a nice flat area with a few trees you could possibly set this up in less than thirty minutes.

Using Natural Terrain

➤ Is there any natural terrain you could use? A cliff wall, very thick bushes, trees, or brush that is impassable could all be used. Other possibilities include man-made structures such as the walls of a lean-to, fence, and or building. Important note: when using an existing structure such as a lean-to, house or building to serve as a wall for the eruv, make sure no part of the structure protrudes over the top of the eruv pole as this would invalidate it.

> The fishing line must connect to a pole that is connected to the existing structure. You can't tie the line directly to a fence or to the side of a cliff.

Guidelines in Setting Up the Poles

> The line should run unobstructed from one pole to the next. It must not be deflected by a tree branch.

> Height should not vary from the top of one pole to the next unless it runs parallel with the terrain, such as up or down a hill.

> Poles should be standing upright. A slight tilt may be okay, but certainly not anything very crooked.

> If the ground is firm you may be able to drive the pole directly into it. Another way to secure it is to prop it between some rocks. A further way is to tie the poles to trees using the cord, though make sure the fishing line does not touch the tree at any point.

> The maximum distance permitted from one lechi to the next depends on whose Halachic opinion you follow, though if you are building a small eruv for a couple of tents and a kitchen area, this should not be an issue.

Connecting the String

- ➤ The line must go directly over the top of the pole. It may not be tied around it. Thus the nail should be in the middle to wrap the line around.

- ➤ The line should not sag or move in the wind.

As mentioned previously, if you are serious about building an eruv while camping, take the time to study the Halachot with a competent rabbi.

Chapter 11: On Shabbat

Friday Night Service

If all members of your group have a similar Jewish background and synagogue habits, you should obviously create a Friday night service suited to the group. But if some are regular synagogue goers and others are unaffiliated, you'll need to give some thought to what kind of service you'd like to run. You could mix the language of the prayers, reading some in Hebrew and some in English. Try some Shlomo Carlebach tunes. Sing 'Lecha Dodi' to the tune of 'She'll be Coming Round the Mountain When She comes,' and get everyone line dancing. Have someone prepare a short piece of Torah, tell a story or perhaps recite a poem about the beauty of G-d in nature. Do give some thought to what will work for your group.

Being out in nature is an opportunity to really connect with our spiritual selves. Many go camping in the first place for this very reason. So use the Friday night service and all of Shabbat to make it a wonderful spiritual outdoor experience as opposed to a day that is just restrictive.

Kiddush and Havdala

❖ *Kiddush Friday night*: ideally should be made on grape juice or wine. If neither are available then kiddush should be made on '*hamotzi*', this being bread, pita, matzah, etc. Recite the normal kiddush and insert the blessing of '*hamotzilechem min ha'aretz*', in place of '*boreiprihagafen.*'

❖ *Kiddush Shabbat day:* differs from Friday night with regards to what kiddush can be made on. Along with grape juice or wine, you may also use drinks such as beer, whiskey, or vodka.

❖ *Havdala:* can be made on grape juice, wine, beer, and also other drinks known as '*chamar medina*' (drinks you would serve to a guest). There are some debates amongst the rabbis as to what constitutes this category; but if you did not have wine, grape juice, or beer, there are plenty of notable rabbis who hold you could make it on tea, coffee, or even orange juice. With regards to using soda, some say yes and some no. If you absolutely have nothing else, make it on soda.

For *besamim* you can use perhaps cinnamon from your cooking kit, find something growing wild that smells nice, or take a few cloves with you. For candles, two small Hanukkah candles is a good lightweight option. Even smaller are the tiny birthday cake candles which will burn for a minute or two. Most compact of all, if weight is a challenge you can strike two large matches together and make the beracha '*boreimeoreiha'aish.*'

Eating Area

According to the Rama (a notable Halachic authority), it is almost impossible to eat without spilling liquid on the ground and people should therefore not have picnics on Shabbat in their own garden. But we can be more lenient when camped in a national park and the like, because there is less of a concern. The problem with accidently spilling liquid in one's own garden is that even though it may not be done on purpose, a person is happy with the outcome because his grass will grow better. This does not apply when you are camped in the middle of nowhere. Either way one should be careful not to spill anything on the ground.

It is also prohibited to feed any wild animal that does not depend on you for its food (actually you should not be feeding anything in the wild at all; but I won't go into a lengthy discussion of why). Keep this in mind as if you are camped in a busy campground area. There is a good chance you will have some bird, squirrel, duck or something hanging around waiting for some food, so remember not to absentmindedly throw anything to them.

Dirty dishes: You can rinse them if you have a washing area set up. If not, place them in a plastic container until after Shabbat.

One dishwashing method used in the outdoors is to rub sand around in a dish until the dish is cleaned. This actually works very well if you are on a beach or in a desert. Dirt is muktzah, but if set aside before Shabbat for a specific use, it is permitted to handle it. However, there is another issue, that if you rub sand in dirty dish you might come to make mud; and making mud is forbidden on Shabbat. Therefore this method of dishwashing should not be used.

Lighting: A simple method that has always worked well for me is to string a line between two trees, around four to five feet high, and then hang a head lamp from it. Set up your eating area under this and you should have plenty of light. Make sure to put fresh batteries in before Shabbat.

Water: Collect enough water before Shabbat; this may be from a tap, river, lake etc. You'll want sufficient water for drinking, washing and cleaning. If you are car camping, bring along some empty water containers to fill, such as soda bottles. For extreme backcountry camping, I'll use a few 'Vapur' bottles. These are collapsible plastic water bottles that weigh next to nothing. You could also fill a hydration pack if you have one large enough.

Techum Shabbat

There is a prohibition on Shabbat to travel, but what constitutes travel?

You may want to do a small hike on Shabbat, so it's important to be familiar with the basics of techum. Techum Shabbat, which literally means 'Shabbat Border,' is the limit set for how far one may travel on Shabbat. Inside a city, village or any place where people live, one can walk around non-stop over the entire Shabbat if one feels like it. The problem is when the city's boundary is left behind and there are no longer any fixed dwellings.

The techum extends for 2000 cubits around a city in every direction. The exact measurement of the cubit is debated to be between 18.9 and 22.7 inches. This equals roughly 3000 feet which equals 0.6 miles or 1 km. Now the average person will walk 1 km on a straight paved road in around 10 to 12 minutes. And obviously if you take a more leisurely stroll or the terrain is uneven this could extend up to around a 20 minute walk. So if you want to take a bit of a nature stroll on Shabbat, pay attention to the distance you are traveling away from your campsite. It is possible that you can take a longer walk if you're doing it in a circular motion around your campsite so if there was a nature trail which circles say around the area where you are camping you may be able to hike for a longer period of time.

But if you want to take a longer hike, then you can make what is called an 'eruv techumin'. This is an act that makes it halachically possible to extend the distance permitted to travel in a specific direction. To make the eruv, you need to place an amount of food that would constitute a meal at a distance of 2000 amot (0.6 miles) from your campsite. Recite the specified beracha and you can then travel a further 2000 amot. Note however that when you return to your campsite, you can no longer travel 2000 amot in the opposite direction as you could before you made the eruv.

Using the eruv techumin can work if there is a specific place you wanted to visit on Shabbat that may be a mile away. As far as going for a general walk, you are probably better off walking in a circular direction around your site.

A few pointers if you are going for a walk: On Shabbat you should not walk near a lake, stream or bog if there is a good chance you will step in and get your clothes wet. This would include walking over a log that is across the water - because you might fall in and come to wring out your wet clothes, a forbidden action. Thus said, the above only applies if you are walking for the sake of walking. If you have a specific place you are going to, then it is not a worry.

Also be careful when tying and untying shoe/boot laces. It is fairly common to have wet laces while camping in most parts of the world other than in a desert. Care should be taken not to tie them too tightly and thus cause the water to wring out. The same with untying.

Tip: keep in mind that even while walking in the techum, you may not carry anything. If you are not carrying a map, water, food etc, you probably don't want to be taking any serious hike.

Mosquitoes

Mosquitoes can be a serious annoyance at any point while camping and even more so on Shabbat when it is forbidden to kill any living thing. It is frustrating when you are trying to go to sleep in a tent and you have a mosquito buzzing around you and you can't kill it. What you do? There are some authorities that hold it is permissible to kill a mosquito because of the diseases which they can carry. This is certainly the case if you are camping somewhere in South America, Southeast Asia or Africa where malaria and other mosquito-carrying deadly diseases exist. In such places, you may according to some opinions be permitted to kill a mosquito buzzing around your tent, because it is a life threatening situation. However in places where mosquitoes do not commonly carry deadly diseases this should not be relied on.

Any sort of bug repellent cream may not be used, though spray and liquid is fine.

You can always burn some mosquito coils around the area where you'll be sitting and eating prior to Shabbat.

Be super vigilant when entering and exiting your tent, making sure not to leave the door open so the mosquitoes won't get in.

It is also permissible to spray repellent in a room (in our case a tent) into the air, provided there are no bugs flying around that it will kill. So you could spray the wall of the tent, which will help keep the bugs away; though I would not recommend this because of the toxic fumes, and also the spray could damage the tent fabric.

I've got a lightweight net that goes over my shoulders, face and head. I use this in situations where there are mosquitoes and I've got no choice but to accept they are going to stay.

If a bee flies into your tent on Shabbat, you should trap it and let it out. Normally trapping is forbidden on Shabbat, but since it's only by force of rabbinic enactment, it is permissible here because they are potentially dangerous to some people. With regards to anything poisonous such as a funnel web spider (I had one in my tent once), black widow, scorpion etc, you may certainly kill it.

Suntan Lotion

Rubbing on lotions on Shabbat is prohibited. Best to have liquid spray-on lotion which won't need any sort of rubbing it into the skin. If it's going to be a hot and sunny day then wear a longsleeved shirt and cover yourself up with a big hat and it shouldn't be necessary to wear suntan lotion.

Smelling Flowers

According to the majority of Halachic opinions, it is permissible to smell flowers and plants connected to the ground. Because they are not considered food, the rabbis were not concerned that one would come to pick them. On the other hand, some opinions hold that flowers should not be smelled. Either way, one should be careful not to break off and pick anything that is attached to the ground.

People often don't realize that there are blessings on smell as well as food. It is important to make the correct blessing when smelling nice plants: '*borehatzeh besamim.*' 'Atzeh,' means 'tree,' and this blessing is made on plants that have a hard stalk and leaves, and last from year to year. Some examples: myrtle, honeysuckle, rose, jasmine, and rosemary. '*Borehisvei besamim*' is made on plants with soft stalks, and on plants that do not last from year to year, such as mint and daffodil. If uncertain which category the plant belongs to, or you are in a garden that has a mixed fragrance of both types of plants, recite a general blessing '*boreiminei besamim.*'

Swimming

When it comes to swimming on Shabbat, all kinds of issues arise, We are afraid of watering the grass with droplets that fall off our bodies when we exit the water, or (if it is a pool) that the water may overflow when entering and water the ground. There is the issue of transporting water on the body when exiting the lake or pool. We are worried we might come to squeeze water out of our hair, a towel, or a bathing suit. Some say that swimming with a swimsuit could be considered laundering; and so on.

It seems that in the times of the Talmud that there were rabbis who permitted swimming in various situations. The ShulchanAruch rules that it is permissible to swim on Shabbat in a pool that is entirely surrounded by walls. However today's Poskim rule that it is not in the spirit of Shabbat. Today the general consensus is that we do not swim. That said, chassidic men who go to the mikvah (ritual immersion) every day will use a lake or ocean on Shabbat though care must still be taken.

In conclusion, on a blistering hot summer's day, you may be okay to let young children swim in a campground pool, because we could also say the heat is a potential danger. The same would apply for adults, depending on the specific individual's ability to cope with the heat.

As for a male adult, here's an idea: you could start going to the mikvah before the trip, and then keep going on Shabbat when you are camping.

Walking on Grass

If you are camping, then there is a good chance you will be walking on grass. One may walk on Shabbat over grass of any kind, whether moist or dry and we don't worry about the risk of cutting or uprooting grass with our shoes. It is also fine to walk barefoot on grass, even though there is a good chance grass will get stuck to the foot and be uprooted from the ground. If grass does stick to the feet, it may not be removed by hand, since the grass is considered muktzah. Rather, you should shake the grass off or rub the foot against a surface to remove it. For example, if your two-year-old runs around barefoot and then comes into the tent, be careful how you brush the grass off her feet.

Drying Out Clothing

Drying out clothes, a tent or a sleeping bag is something that often needs to get done on a camping trip. But hanging up clothes to dry on Shabbat is prohibited.

Clothing that is wet when Shabbat comes in, even if only partially wet, is considered muktzah and may not be handled on Shabbat even after it has dried. If, however you are in a hot, dry climate where you know that the clothing will definitely dry before Shabbat is over, there is room to permit its use on Shabbat when already dry.

An item that became wet on Shabbat, though it has the status of muktzah while wet, it is no longer considered muktzah once it dries, and may be handled. Note that wet clothing may not be hung up as you would normally hang clothes to dry, as it will appear to have been laundred on Shababt.

In a home setting, you would mostly dry clothes by hanging them on a line or a drying rack. You might sometimes place an item over a chair to dry, but this would not be considered the norm. So on Shabbat, one can throw wet clothing over a chair. In the outdoors there are two normal ways to dry clothes: on a string tied between trees, or throwing the item directly over a branch. So on Shabbat, neither of these methods may be used. Thus said, it is still common to dry clothes over a rock, on a picnic table, or even directly on the ground in the sun. So care should be taken with how you deal with any wet items.

If an item was already dry before Shabbat but left hanging, it may be removed from the line. Taking clothes down from a line is permitted and we need not worry that people will think you washed the item on Shabbat, according to the ShulchanAruch.

When camping, it is important to be make sure that the line you are removing from is not connected directly to a tree. (See section on 'Bear Bags')

The type of drying prohibited on Shabbat only applies in the case of natural materials, because they are considered to absorb liquids. Plastics, rubber, synthetics and the like are treated with more leniency. For example a plastic rain poncho, since it does not absorb any liquid, may be shaken off vigorously and hung up in the normal way. Care should be taken though not to shake it in an area where the liquid will directly fall to the ground. The same would apply to a sleeping bag that got soaked at night. If it is fully synthetic, you may move it into the sun, or place it on perhaps a picnic table to dry. This is good news for campers, as most high tech clothing is 100% synthetic. However if it is a mix, such as a pair of socks made of 80% synthetic materials and 20% wool, they may not be hung up to dry.

Clothing that got wet on Shabbat may be put on again on Shabbat if you have no other clothing.

Example 1: Before going to sleep on Friday night, you left your tzitzit on a bench outside. From 4:00-5:00 am it rains, and when you get up your tzitzit are wet. If they are your only pair you may wear them. But if you have a second pair you could wear that; and then if later in the day the sun comes out and dries the first pair, you may put them back on.

Example 2: Friday night you get a big storm which leaks into the tent (probably because it was not set up right) and you wake up in a puddle. If your sleeping bag is 100% synthetic, you can bring it outside (provided you are in an Eruv enclousure) to dry in the sun and use later in the day. If the sleeping bag is of natural materials (cotton, down, wool etc.), you will need to make a fire after Shabbat and dry it off.

Important note: fire may never be used on Shabbat to dry off clothing. Wearing wet clothes and standing near a fire with the intention of drying off is prohibited.

Chapter 12 : Winter Camping

For the sake of this chapter, I will define winter camping as camping with or without the presence of snow, where the temperature at night will drop below freezing and will rise a few degrees above freezing by day. This is moderate winter camping.

Two important issues arise when it comes to keeping Shabbat in winter camping:

1) The need to have non-frozen liquids to drink, preferably warm.

2) The need to keep the body warm during the day without conducting any major activity such as skiing, backpacking, shelter construction, ice climbing and so on.

With desert winter camping, in some places, the temperature may drop well below zero, but will quickly heat up in the morning and therefore the issue of staying warm by day and having water to drink is not a factor.

In 'moderate winter camping' where the sun comes out by day and the temperatures rises a bit at least a few degrees above freezing, food should thaw so that it is not a solid chunk of ice, and even if you can't have a hot drink, liquids in bottles should also thaw out. You will also be able to keep warmish in the sun.

The biggest challenge is staying warm throughout the day on Saturday. As just mentioned, winter camping usually involves an activity done by day such as walking, skiing, or climbing, etc. This keeps the body moving and warm. If you are unable to do much activity and further unable to heat liquids, Shabbat can be a long cold day. I'd only recommend camping out in extreme winter conditions over Shabbat if you are forced to because of an extended trip such as skiing to the north or south poles! (or mountain climbing - see more below).

The important thing is to avoid getting cold in the first place. Be sure to put on a hat and extra pair of socks. Change out of a sweaty thermal top or wet snow pants. Do this all *before* you get cold, not after.

Wearing Gloves

There is an issue of wearing gloves on Shabbat. We are afraid one may come to remove them to shake hands and then carry them in a public domain.

It's probably fine to wear gloves in winter camping, because a) if you are wearing them you probably really need them, and b) the likelihood of meeting an old friend with whom to shake hands while you are camped in middle of nowhere is not high.

Food: In cold weather camping, it is important to eat a good amount of protein and fat-based food. Eating protein in the evening will help keep the body warm through the night and then eat protein again in the morning to stay warm during the day. Friday evening you should be able to eat a hot meal as you usually would. Cook the food so that it is very hot. Wrap it a towel and put in a sleeping bag and it should stay hot long enough for you to light Shabbat candles and daven before eating (and it will also warm your sleeping bag!)

Here are a few tips with regards to food:

- ❖ Tuna in sachets are good sources of protein to eat by day because you can place them inside a jacket and they thaw quickly.
- ❖ Nuts are a good food and edible even when frozen; but you can defrost a handful by putting them in an inside pocket. Be careful not to walk out of an eruv with food in your pockets.
- ❖ Butter is a super food for winter camping and is taken on virtually all serious winter expeditions. Spread butter on your Challah at the Friday night meal, eat some on crackers for breakfast and have some with Challah again at kiddush lunch, and it will help keep you warm. Basically add butter to everything. A wrapped piece of butter can easily be placed inside your jacket pocket to melt. Alternatively, we lose most of our body heat through our head, so if you want to defrost some butter/nuts etc. place it under your hat!
- ❖ Some food can be kept in your sleeping bag overnight to keep it from freezing and to eat when you wake up. You need to be careful that you don't roll on top of it and end up sleeping on the food. Not only might you squash it, but this will also create a religious problem, as spiritual impurity that descends on the body at night is passed on to the food and makes it no longer suitable to be eaten.

- ❖ Unless you enjoy frozen bread, you're better off with Matzah.

- ❖ Liquids: The challenge with camping in below-zero degree temperatures is having drinking water on Shabbat. Normally you would melt snow and ice for water. Friday evening should not be a problem as you can melt snow before Shabbat. To prepare water for Shabbat day, you will need a few quality thermoses. Fill them with hot water before Shabbat and, except in extremely cold conditions, they won't be hot by Shabbat day but should still stay liquid. As for making kiddush by day, you could boil some grape juice before Shabbat and put it in a thermos: it should still be in liquid form (not frozen) on Shabbat morning.

- ❖ Wrap any thermos that contains hot liquid you intend to drink the next day in a towel and keep it in your sleeping bag over night. This will keep its contents (and you) warmer for longer.

- ❖ You can store extra water for the next day by placing a bottle of water upside down in the snow. Keeping the bottle inverted will prevent the lid from freezing, as any ice that forms will form towards the top. Remember to mark the spot, perhaps with a ski pole.

- ❖ Hot liquids: Be careful when pouring hot liquids into plastic water bottles. Apart from melting the plastic, as the water cools it will contract and cause the bottle to deform. A good metallic thermos is best for storing hot liquids.

Washing Hands

In a snowy zone, it is permissible to wash hands, either in the morning when waking up or before eating bread. by dipping them in the snow, if there is a pile large enough to cover both hands.

Going to the Toilet

Try not to urinate on snow because it can melt the snow, which is an issue on Shabbat. If you can, find some rocks or fallen trees. If you have no option then just urinate on snow.

With regards to defecating, going to the toilet in a hole made in the snow is not good, because when the snow melts the excrement will be sitting on top of the ground. If you can find an area of dirt you may be able to dig a hole, depending on how frozen the ground is. Keep in mind though that even if you prepare a hole before Shabbat, if it snows during the night you may not find the hole.

One method is to go to the toilet over some newspaper, then roll it up and place it inside a double layer of zip lock bags. You may also add some kitty litter to absorb moisture and make the waste more transportable. Then take it out with you and dispose. If you are car camping then it is good to put together a camp toilet as described earlier in the book in the section on going to the toilet.

Wet Clothing

With snow camping, wet clothes, such as wet gloves, boot liners, snow pants and so on will be inevitable. Care must be taken, since things may not be dried out on Shabbat near a fire or gas stove. It is common practice in such camping to dry boot liners and gloves in the evening near a gas stove so the moisture in them does not freeze overnight. Since you cannot do this, if you plan on getting wet, it is a good idea to have extra gloves, socks etc. on hand; basically any clothing items you may get wet.

Dealing with Snow

One is allowed to walk upon snow on Shabbat without concern that doing so will cause shoe tracks to be imprinted in the snow, or that snow will come to melt due to walking on it.

Wearing snow shoes (even if there is no eruv) is alright on Shabbat if you need them to get somewhere.

Playing with snow:

There are three issues:
1) Snow may be muktzah.
2) Squeezing to make the snow balls.
3) Building.

Adults should not partake in any snow ball fights. Young kids should be shown other activities to do, though if they do get into a snow ball fight it is not necessary to stop them, provided it is done in an eruv.

Building a snow man should not be done on Shabbat, as it comes under the heading of the prohibition of building.

Shovelling snow:

There is a dispute with regards to whether snow is considered muktzah and is there a difference between snow that fell before Shabbat or on Shabbat. There is also an issue of tircha (strenuous work) which should not be done on Shabbat.

It is best not to shovel snow unless you have a good reason to do so. In winter camping, after a heavysnow fall at night, you will often need to move the snow from around your entrance to the tent or snow cave. You may also need to remove snow from the tent to prevent it from collapsing. This should be fine to do. Even without an eruv you can move the snow a couple of feet without a problem. It's also good to designate a shovel before Shabbat to be used on Shabbat to clear snow with.

Eruv

Snow brings some new aspects to eruv building. A suggestion is to build an eruv with ski poles. Fasten an upright screw on the top of the handle using packing tape. Then place the poles in the snow and use fishing line, wrapped around the screws to connect them. Make sure that when they are driven into the snow that they will still be 10 tefachim high (around three feet).

You could also build a snow wall, which if you are camped in an extreme environment with lots of snow is something you'd probably do anyway. This is usually done by cutting blocks of snow and stacking them around your camp site. You could combine a snow wall and a few connected ski poles to make an eruv.

Chapter 13: Camping at High Altitude

The definition of high altitude here is anything above 3000 meters. The two main challenges are staying warm and staying hydrated. This is more or less the same two issues you will have with winter camping. However at altitude it can be more dangerous. There is less oxygen in the air and thereby lower oxygen levels in the blood. Because of this decrease, the body prioritizes circulation to vital organs, which means that extremities become colder quicker than they would at sea level. Also, because of the lower air pressure, water evaporates faster, which can lead to dehydration.

Staying Hydrated

In winter camping, the air is dry and it is important to drink a lot. People often don't realize for example that Antarctica is a desert. It is, in fact, the driest place on earth, as there is little or no precipitation from the air. When camped even in the cold winter snow, drinking lots of liquid is critical. If you make sure to be well hydrated before Shabbat, then even if you only have a liter or two over Shabbat, with general winter camping this should not be an issue. You can have a few hot bowls of soup after Shabbat and plenty of tea at Sunday breakfast. At worst the body will get slightly dehydrated.

At altitude, it is dangerous not to drink; and the higher one is, the more critical ingesting fluids becomes. Therefore it is important to have a system where you will have enough liquid over Shabbat. This can be taken care of by filling a few extra hot water thermoses, provided you are able to carry the weight.

Staying Warm

Make sure your clothes and sleeping bag are adequate for keeping warm over a day of inactivity.

At altitude there is a strong possibility of extreme weather. Heavy snowfall and strong winds can collapse a tent, making it necessary to fix on Shabbat. As mentioned previously in the book, it can be very helpful here not only to have a non-Jew with you but to actually share the tent with the non-Jew, who will be able to fix the shelter for his or her own benefit. Remember to help out later with something extra, so that your tent partner does not just think you are lazy and you don't make a chillul Hashem.

If you are on a guided trip and using a tent belonging to a non-Jewish trekking company, then it is fine for the guides and porters to do anything they wish to fix the tent, and similarly to fix any equipment belonging to the company.

As to building an eruv at altitude - it won't work, and if it did it probably won't last long. You'll need to set your camp up such that you should not need to carry. That said, at altitude there is not much carrying done anyway between your tent and the outside. Everything besides perhaps skis and ski poles should be kept in your tent. However it is also possible that where you camp may not need an eruv to begin with, for example if it is a small space surrounded by rock walls and cliffs.

Note: The higher in elevation one is, the later Shabbat will arrive because the sunset can be viewed further on the horizon.

Chapter 14: Shabbat Activities

It's good to come prepared with interesting and exciting activities that you can do on a Shabbat afternoon, particularly in the summer when it can be long. If you are camping with children or with friends, then planning like this will provide more interest and a more enjoyable experience. This is so much more important nowadays, when many people have forgotten what they did before we spent all our time glued to the screens of our computer, phone, tablet etc.

Here are some ideas:

Acting out the parasha: This can be a lot of fun when you are in a group of people. Divide the Torah portions and get groups or individuals to act out each aliya. This will provide an exciting and interesting way for people to get involved with studying the weekly Torah portion.

Take time to pray: Because you're not confined to any sort of synagogue which is running on a schedule, you may find that you enjoy taking the extra time to look more into your prayer and meditate on the meaning of the words. Perhaps compose a tune and sing it while you pray. You are in no rush.

*Discussions:*Think of some interesting topics and maybe get some information off the web. Things that will make for a good long discussion, such as morality, evolution, and the meaning of life. Taking topics from the weekly parasha is a great way to get discussions going. A key to making discussions work is to raise a certain situation and ask people what they would have done themselves, how they feel about the situation and why they feel that way.

Study first aid: Most first aid can be practiced on Shabbat, aside from tying bandages. You can practice CPR, talk about dealing with snakebites, burns, frostbite, shock, and heat exhaustion; and you can practice carrying injured people (if you have an eruv). Play out first aid situations and how you would deal with them.

Read: Having a good book is a must to help pass along Shabbat afternoon. Perhaps bring a book that you can read together and take turns.

Study about Shabbat: Why not spend time learning and discussing the laws of Shabbat. You could read straight from the KitzurShulchanAruch (Abridged Code of Jewish Law), or alternatively, get one of the more contemporary books on the subject. A good book that covers practical Halachic observance. and is also entertaining, is *'Do You Know Hilchos Shabbos?'* by Rabbi Michoel Fletcher. You can also find books that deal more with the spiritual essence of Shababt such as *'7th Heaven -Celebrating Shabbat with RebbeNachman of Breslov,'* by Moshe Mykoff.

Tell stories: Have a contest for who can tell the best story. It could be real or made up.

Map and compass: Practicing reading maps and developing orienteering skills is important to a camper. If you are going to engage in this activity on Shabbat, keep in mind that you should not study a map to plan your walks for the next week, nor do any math that relates to calculating distances, elevation and direction.

Card and board games: Chess, checkers, backgammon, Uno, Bananagrams, a deck of cards etc. They are easy to pack and can be slipped into backpacks for easy carrying. Rolling dice can be a problem on Shabbat, so games that require them should be avoided, or you can try and find an alternative to dice, for example making a stack of cards with numbers on them which people pick up at random. Games like charades and 'I Spy' are ideal because you don't have to bring anything with you to play them.

Charades: A word guessing game, where one or multiple players act out a word or phrase and the others try to guess it. The idea is to do the acting without any verbal clues. You can give this a Jewish twist by acting out biblical personalities or a saying from PirkeiAvot (Ethics of Our Fathers).

Theatersports and improvisation: There is a huge range of games that can be played. Google "Breakaway Theatre Sports pdf" to find a free downloadable book with enough ideas to keep going all Shabbat afternoon. For more ideas, google "Theatersports". You can also give some thought to how to give the games a Jewish twist.

Enjoying nature: Part of the joy of camping is being closer to nature. Think how you can arrange activities such as: bird watching, animal watching, stargazing, wild plant identification {though do not touch).

Chapter 15: MelavaMalka

Motzei Shabbat is an incredibly spiritual time when we can channel the holiness of Shabbat to shine into the entire week. Take the time, if you can, to sing a beautiful havdala. Reb Shlomo Carlebach is known to have composed some beautiful tunes for havdala. Check on YouTube. If you've got anyone with an instrument, have them bring it out and play along.

Following havdala, you could have everyone switch on their headlamps to strobe/flashing mode. Then have an impromptu dance/disco as you sing songs like 'Eliyahu Hanavi'. It's a lot of fun!

Following havdala, many have the custom to have a beautiful meal with singing and words of Torah, just like a Shabbat meal. This meal is known as MelavaMalka as well as 'Se'udatad'DavidMalkaMeshicha', the meal of David, King Messiah. At a MelavaMalka, one should eat bread and a hot dish; preferably something freshly made in honor of the meal - could be a potato in the camp fire, or a hot dog etc.

There is a story in the Talmud about Rabbi Abbahu. At the conclusion of each Shabbat, Rabbi Abbahu would instruct his family to slaughter a calf and he would then eat one of the kidneys. At one point his son asked him why they bothered to slaughter a new calf when they could just save a kidney from the calf that they had slaughtered before Shabbat for the Shabbat meals. Rabbi Abbahu agreed and they set aside some meat from the Shabbat calf to be eaten at MelavaMalka. But a lion came and devoured one of his calves, and he saw that nothing was gained by saving from the Shabbat meat. The moral of the story is, try not to just eat leftovers, make something fresh, even just popcorn.

During MelavaMalka, the Chassidic custom is to tell a story about the Baal Shem Tov. Rabbi Yisroel (Israel) ben Eliezer, often called 'Baal Shem Tov' or 'Besht' for short, was a Jewish mystical rabbi. He is considered to be the founder of Chassidic Judaism. There are many fascinating stories about him and they certainly make for great campfire stories. Go to Chabad.org and search Baal Shem Tov, and you will find many wonderful tales. You can also tell general stories of great Chassidic mastersand you can find some good ones here: http://www.nishmas.org/htmldocs/stories.html

I've always found that a beautiful Jewish story around a campfire after Shabbat is memorable. Certainly have fun, tell jokes, do some wild dancing, and perform a few funny skits, but throw in some Jewish spirituality as well and it will be a lot more special.

The Jewish Campfire

One of my favorite all time resources is the 'Jewish Camp Song Book' put out by Tzivos Hashem. You can find it online as a free downloadable word document. Search 'Tzivos Hashem Camp Song Book.'

Some of the songs may not resonate with you personally, being too religious based or geared towards a Chabad Lubavitch community. However, there is still a lot of wonderful material in the book. It's well worth having a look through it to find material you can use. Also keep in mind that many of the songs can be recited as poetry if you don't know the tunes.

Another good resource is the NCSY (National Council of Synagogue Youth) bencher. It contains a good variety of Jewish songs taken from text in Jewish prayers and Tanach. If you have a group of Hebrew speakers, perhaps print out a list of popular Israel folk songs like, '*BashanaHaba'a*', '*YerushalayimShelZahav*', '*HavaNagila*' etc.

Songs from 'Fiddler on The Roof' like 'Sunrise Sunset,' 'If I Were a Rich Man' and others can work well around the campfire, depending on your audience.

You can be creative and try songs like 'Chad Gadya' from the Pesach Seder. Have everyone make the appropriate sounds of the animals and other things mentioned in the song. You can follow this with "Who Knows One?" (EchadMiYode'a) and more.

It's nice to get everyone involved. One way to do this is to go around the circle, and everyone has one of three options:

1) Tell a story

2) Start a song

3) Start a discussion on a topic of interest.

Some people may use the term 'Kumzits,' to refer to a Jewish campfire sing-along. Kumzits is a compound-word in Hebrew derived from Yiddish, meaning "come and sit." Having a Kumzits has grown in popularity over the years, and is a great opportunity to infuse some spirituality into your group. Usually slow, moving songs are sung with compositions by the likes of Dveykus and Shlomo Carlebach.

This is a list of what I believe to be many of the most popular Kumzits tunes. You can search YouTube with the song name and will probably find most if you wanted to learn them.

1. *V'atahBunimShiruLamelech* (Yeedle)
2. *AchasSha'altiMei'eis Ha-shem*(Dveykus)
3. *ShifchiKamayimLeebeich* (Carlebach)
4. *Na'arHayeesee Gam Zakanti*(Dveykus)
5. *AniMa'aminBe'emunaSh'leima...BeviasHamashiach (various tunes)*
6. *LashemHaaretz* (Yitzchak Fuchs)
7. *VuatemHadvekim...(*Baruch Chait*)*
8. *Chamol...(*YigalCalek*)*
9. *RachemB'chasdecha Al AmchaTzureinu (various tunes)*
10. *AcheinuKolBeis Yisroel* (Abie Rotenberg &Doody Rosenberg)
11. *Hamalach...(*Doody Rosenberg*)*
12. *KolHaolamKuloGesherTzarMe'od*(Carlebach)
13. *Tov LehodosLashem (various tunes)*
14. *VezakeiniLegadel* (Boruch Levine)
15. *MeeHa'ishHachafetzChaim* (Baruch Chait)
16. *BilvaviMishkanEvneh*(Dveykus)
17. *L'ma'anAchaiV'rei'ai* (Carlebach)
18. *Unuh Hashem KeeAneeAvd'chu*(Carlebach)
19. *Pischu Li Sha'areiTzedek* (Carlebach)
20. *BarcheinuAveenuKulanuK'echad* (Carlebach)
21. *Gam KeeEileichB'geiTzalmaves (various tunes)*
22. *LuleiSoraschaSha'ashu'ai* (Carlebach)
23. *Eliyahu Hanavee* (Carlebach)
24. *Hadran* (Hillel Kapnick)
25. *ImEshkacheichYerushalayim*(various tunes)

Chapter 16: Special Berachot

If you are spending time camping there is a good chance you will have the opportunity to make some special berachot.

On Seeing a Rainbow

"Baruch atah Ado-naielo-heinumelech ha-olam, zocherhaberitvene'emanbivritov'kaiyambema'amaro."
Blessed are You, Lord our G-d, King of the universe, who remembers the covenant, and is faithful to His covenant, and keeps His promise.

According to the Torah, the rainbow came into being after the flood of Noah. G-d showed Noah a rainbow and said, 'In the future if I am upset at the world I will show a rainbow.' Thus, seeing a rainbow is not a good omen: one should not point it out to a friend if they do see it.

Flowering Fruit Trees

"Baruch atah Ado-naielo-heinumelech ha-olamshelochisarb'olomokloomu'vorobobriostovosv'ilonostovosl'hanosbohembneiodom."
Blessed are You, Lord our G-d, King of the universe, who did not cause anything to be lacking in His world, and created within it pleasant creations and pleasant trees, to bring pleasure to man.

This blessing may be recited only once a year and preferably in the Hebrew month of Nisan and when viewing several flowering fruit trees together. There are some opinions that hold that the blessing may be said later if you did not make the blessing the first time you saw the blossoms, and can even be said in other months besides Nissan.

Shooting Star, Comet, Tornado, Hurricane, Lightning, Landscape

"Baruch atah Ado-naielo-heinumelech ha-olamosehma'asehvereshis."
Blessed are You, G-d, our Lord, King of the Universe, Who re-enacts the work of creation.

Shooting star, comet:The blessing on the shooting star (scientific name: meteor) is only made once per night, and on a comet once in thirty days. A shooting star is a large rock that is burning up as it moves. It leaves a tail of light that lasts for a fraction of a second. Virtually on any clear dark night you should be able to see a shooting star, possibly a hundred of them. A comet is a ball of ice, water and gas and is very rare. Chances are you will only see a few in your lifetime. When they come, they remain visible for a much longer period of time as they travel across the sky.

Tornado, hurricane:Hopefully you won't see any hurricanes or tornadoes when you are camping, but if you do, you can make the blessing.

Lightning:A blessing is made on lightning only when it is part of a storm. Not all lightning is the same. In Australia I have often seen lightning shows go on for hours, with lightning flashing impressively across the sky; but this is heat-based lightning and a blessing is not made on this.

The blessing should be made once per storm and recited within threeseconds. So this is an important beracha to know by heart, as there is no time to look up the words.

Landscape: There is a special blessing recited over five types of impressive landscapes: seas, rivers, mountains, hills, and deserts.

When it comes to mountains, the blessing is only made when seeing a very high and famous mountain. There are fourteen mountains in the world over 8000 meters high. Three of the most famous are Everest, K2, and Annapurna, though you could certainly make the blessing on any of the fourteen. There are the seven summits i.e. the highest mountain on every continent. You could make the beracha on six of the seven, except for Australia (Kosciuszko is not much of a mountain). Other famous mountains could include, for instance: Mt. Blanc, The Matterhorn, Mt. Rainier, and Mt. Whitney.

The same idea applies to seeing a major river like the Amazon or the Nile as well as a landscape like the Grand Canyon, or the Sahara Desert. The idea here is, that you feel inspired with awe and want to pay tribute to Hashem.

On Hearing Thunder

"Baruch atah Ado-naielo-heinumelech ha-olamshekochou'gevuratomaleiolam."

Blessed are You, G-d, our Lord, King of the Universe, whose strength and might fills the world.

As in the case of lightning, this blessing is only made once per storm.

The two blessings (one on lightning and one on thunder) are recited only if you first see the lightning and then hear the thunder, or vice versa. If you experience them both simultaneously, you just say one of the blessings, whichever one you wish, and the one will cover both.

Chapter 17: PikuachNefesh

'PikuachNefesh' is the concept of saving a life. On Shabbat, anything may be done to save a life. There are many complicated Halachot involved in this area which assess the seriousness of the situation. For example; when you should you ask a non-Jew or a minor (if such in the vicinity) to do something versus doing it yourself. Further, should you do the melacha in an abnormal way, thus minimising the desecration of Shabbat, or perform the action in its regular manner? With the above in mind, **when there is any doubt at all, it is forbidden to be stringent when it comes to pikuachnefesh**. If you think there is danger to life, then do what has to be done.

Some may say: "How can you go camping on Shabbat if it can potentially put you in a position where you will need to break Shabbat due to pikuachnefesh?"

I meet people who are scared of the outdoors and they think it is filled with dangers: snakes, bears, lightning strikes, bush fires, falling trees, storms, and forests filled with monsters. But many things in life can be safe or dangerous depending on how you do it. Staying home can be dangerous. Our modern homes, filled with electrical appliances and outlets, glass windows, toilets, bathtubs, power tools, toxic cleaning supplies, sharp furniture corners, book shelves, medicine cabinets and so on, can make our home the most dangerous place to be in. Falling down steps, slipping in the bathtub or on a mopped floor, poisoning from medicines and cleaning supplies, burns and fires, and suffocation - thousands die in their homes every year by accident, and it's known that most accidents occur in the home. But we take measures to ensure that our homes are as safe as possible.

In the same vein, camping over Shabbat does not have to entail putting oneself in a potential dangerous situation where one would need to rely on pikuachnefesh. Accidents can, G-d forbid, happen anywhere; but, provided you are organized properly you should not have any while camping. When dealing with pikuachnefesh, it is important to know the difference between a biblical prohibition and rabbinic one. It is always preferable to break a rabbinical one over a biblical one. Knowing these differences requires a vast amount of study and is beyond the scope of this book, but here is one example as to how this could apply:

Someone has an asthma attack and needs an inhaler. There is one in a car right next to you, but the car is locked and if you open the car doors, this will turn on the car lights. There is also an inhaler a minute's walk away in a campsite office, but this would mean having to carry it without an eruv. You don't want to move the person to the office as this could exacerbate their asthma. If the person knows his or her own limits (as often in the case of asthmatics) and feels able to hold off an extra two minutes, it is better to get the inhaler from outside of the eruv than to turn on the car lights.

As a general rule, if the situation is not life threatening but is causing extreme discomfort and/ or pain, try to have a non-Jew do the melacha if possible.

Any injury which, though not life threatening, is vital to one's future survival, such as the loss of a limb, eyesight or use of a vital organ, is considered pikuahnefesh. If you are interested in the subject, a good book is 'HilchosRefuah on Shabbos - Medical Care on Shabbos,' by Rabbi Yosef B. Simon.

If one took measures to save a life because they believed there was a danger, and then later learned that there was in fact no danger to the person's life, they have not desecrated Shabbat and should by no means feel bad.

Here Are Some Examples of How Shabbat Would Be Taken into Consideration:

1. *A person, G-d forbid, was injured and needs to be carried a few hundred meters to where a helicopter would be able to collect them.* If the helicopter will not arrive for a half hour or so, then you should carry the person slowly, stopping every few feet, so as not to carry more than four amot (cubits) or about 6 feet at a time. However if the helicopter will be there in a few minutes then certainly move the victim as quickly as possible so as to receive medical treatment without any delay. The general rule: minimize melacha only as long as it will not slow down the treatment of the victim.

2. *It's Saturday morning and you have an emergency. You carry your phone up to the top of a hill where you can get a signal to call for help. Help is now on the way. Can you carry your phone back with you? and if it was originally off, can you switch it back off to preserve battery?* This could depend on whether there is another phone available in the group and whether the battery will last for the duration of Shabbat if not turned off.

3. *Someone has succumbed to heatstroke and requires help.* Firstly, move them to a shady spot if they can not move by themselves. Next, you need to determine how severe is the situation. Will it be enough to give them a drink and let them relax in the shade, or is the situation more critical? Perhaps you are camped near a river with cold water which you could collect, soak a towel and use it to cool the person off? This will probably involve carrying and squeezing. Or will it be enough to just carry up some water and drip it lightly onto the affected person, so as not to squeeze on Shabbat?

True Story: *We were camped in a forest in Israel. While we sat eating our Friday night meal, a scorpion stung someone. The person started feeling intense pain and the affected area began to swell. We wanted to locate the scorpion to identify it, as some scorpions are deadly and can kill their victim in minutes, while others will just cause tremendous pain, depending on the individual who is stung.*

A hanging flashlight that was already on was taken from the area where we were eating (thus not having to turn on a new light). The scorpion was found, killed, and placed in a container. Someone then called someone else who they knew could identify the scorpion via description. We concluded that it was not one of the deadly ones. The phone was then switched off to preserve battery life in case we had to make a call in a few hours. We monitored the victim for the next few hours, checking his heart rate, his breathing and the swelling. He was not feeling great but it was not life threatening. The next morning, he was weak but otherwise fine.

Doing Things to Prevent PikuachNefesh Being Necessary in the First Place

Situations can arise in the outdoors where measures need to be taken to prevent danger escalating in the first place. When in the outdoors, you should drink before you get thirsty and stay warm before you get cold. This is a very simple concept that is often overlooked.

The best lifeguard is not the one who saves a dozen people. The best lifeguard is the one who doesn't need to save anyone in the first place, bymaking sure nothing goes wrong to begin with.

With regards to Shabbat, one needs to be aware of what must be done to prevent a life-threatening situation. For example: You are camped with a group of people and the temperatures hit over 40 degrees Celsius. A suggestion is for people to go swimming, though in a controlled manner. This would be a preventative measure from having to deal with someone getting heat stroke. A second example: A storm starts to blast your tent and water begins to soak through. If things worsen, there could be a threat of hypothermia. Don't wait until it's too late. Figure out what minimal melacha should be done to prevent a situation from deteriorating.

Chapter 18: General Camping Tips

This book is about camping on Shabbat, and I've tried to avoid giving general camping information. You should only go camping on Shabbat if you already have some camping experience. You should be comfortable with the basics of pitching a tent, making a fire, cooking on a camp stove, first aid and so on.

However, I've decided to include here a list of twenty-five tips that even a camper with some experience could still appreciate. These are things often overlooked or forgotten, most of which are important to camping on Shabbat.

General Tips

1. Set your tent up at home before heading out to make sure everything is there.
2. Bring at least one more pair of socks than what you think you will need.
3. Remember to bring a can opener if you are bringing canned food.
4. Pack extra batteries for your flashlight.
5. Put a tarp under your tent, it will save the floor and keep you dry.
6. Buy good quality gear to begin with if you plan on camping for a while.
7. Take a warmer sleeping bag than you think you will need, or an extra blanket.
8. Bring some firewood along with you if you are car camping.

9. Take the time to carefully remove all sticks and rocks before setting up your tent.

10. Make sure your ground sheet does not extend out from under your tent - if it rains you will wake up in a puddle.

11. Get a headlamp if you don't already have one. With it you can use both hands.

12. Create a camping checklist and follow it when you are packing.

13. Remember to take your shoes off before getting into the tent. Newbie campers are often lazy with this.

14. Break in your hiking shoes before you go for a long hike! It takes a few weeks to get boots to mold to your feet.

15. Don't bring food into your tent unless you are camped in Antarctica where there are no animals or bugs to visit you for a meal.

16. Pack a few extra tent pegs. They come in handy after you've bent or broken a few.

17. Bring duct tape - important for emergency repairs.

18. If your tent needs the seams sealed, it's good to do it *before* it's raining!

19. Have a good first aid kit and know how to use its contents.

20. Always close your tent when you leave it; this will keep bugs and rain out.

21. Clean up your site before you leave and then clean it up again (since you may have missed something).

22. Avoid touching the walls of your tent when they are wet.

23. Pack a compass to check which way to daven.

24. If it's cold at night, sleep with a hat on. Also put on warm clothing before you get cold.

25. Bring two forms of fire-starting equipment i.e. matches and a lighter.

Shabbat Camping Packing List

These are suggestions of items you should be taking along to add to your packing list

___Challot/Matzah

___Grape juice/wine/beer

___Extra water/container/thermos

___Tallit/Tefillin/Siddur

___Chumash/Tanach/Copy of Parasha, Haftora

___Zemirot booklets/copies of songs

___Candles/Candle holders

___Matches/lighter

___Havdala candle/besamim (spice)

___Shabbat clothes

___Shabbat book/s to read

___Board games/general games/cards

___Eruv kit

___Tissues/torn toilet paper

___Glow sticks/extra headlamp/batteries

Closing

Thank you for taking the time to read this book. Please G-d I hope you have many wonderful and spiritual experiences in the outdoors over Shabbat. The more you camp, the better your skills will become, and with that you will find that camping on Shabbat no longer provides a challenge. Rather, it is a relaxing experience that leaves you spiritually recharged.

There is nowhere in the Torah that says, 'Thou must spend the Sabbath in a big noisy polluted city.' Shabbat is a day to relax; yet the chaos around us does not appear to want to relax. Today more than ever, with the pull of screens from computers, tablets, phones, and so on, for many of us the arrival of Shabbat catches us switching off our screens at the last minute, taking a frantic shower and struggling to stay awake at the Friday night table. Then Shabbat day comes and we want to sleep in, yet we drag ourselves to Shul.

As Rabbi Nachman of Breslov says, "When a person prays in the field, the grass prays with him." For some people a Friday service in the outdoors singing 'Lecha Dodi' ('Come my Beloved Shabbat Queen') is an incredibly powerful spiritual experience.

Sometimes camping has been at the cost of not having a minyan and therefore not being able to read from a Torah. On the other hand, there are many times I've camped with a Torah. I certainly agree that a minyan with a Torah is very important. Thus said, we must keep in mind the purpose of going to Shul in the first place is to have a spiritual experience. It is not just to perform ritual.

Yes, ritual is of absolute importance, but if we try to keep ritual practice with no spiritual connection it does not last. A person needs to take time to reconnect to their spiritual self.

If anyone thinks otherwise, I would argue about the countless Tzadikim who very often prayed alone. We may not be Tzadikim but we still need time to reconnect, and if an occasional camping trip will strengthen your yiddishkeit, then do it. When you sit around on Shabbat afternoon as the sun sets and the birds, and crickets begin their chirping, you can join in and sing songs of praise to Hashem and feel a sense of ruchniyot (G-dliness). Cherish that experience and embrace it. Bring it back with you.

The Essence of Shabbat

G-d created the world in six days and rested on Shabbat, the seventh day, as it says in Genesis 2:1-3:

> *'Heaven and earth, and all their components, were completed. With the seventh day, G-d finished all the work (melacha) that He had done. He ceased on the seventh day from all the work (melacha) that He had been doing. G-d blessed the seventh day, and He declared it to be holy, for it was on this day that G-d ceased from all the work (melacha) that He had been creating to function.'*

By stopping work on Shabbat, G-d showed that the world is complete and lacks nothing. We as Jews are similarly commanded to cease any acts of creation (melachot). When we do this, we acknowledge that all of G-d's creation is perfect and does not need any human input.

The commandment to keep Shabbat as a day of rest is repeated many times in the Torah. Its importance is also stressed in Shemot 31:12-17

> *'And the LORD spoke unto Moses, saying: 'Verily you shall keep My Sabbaths, for it is a sign between Me and you throughout your generations, that you may know that I am the LORD who sanctifies you. Ye shall keep the Sabbath therefore, for it is holy unto you; every one that profanes it shall surely be put to death; for whosoever does any work (melacha—מְלָאכָה) therein, that soul shall be cut off from among his people. Six days shall work be done; but on the seventh day is a Sabbath of solemn rest, holy to the LORD; whosoever does any work in the Sabbath day, he shall surely be put to death. Wherefore the children of Israel shall keep the Sabbath, to observe the Sabbath throughout their generations, for a perpetual covenant. It is a sign between Me and the children of Israel for ever; for in six days the LORD made heaven and earth, and on the seventh day He ceased from work and rested.'*

The Torah commands us to rest from work on the Sabbath but what exactly is work?

The word the Torah uses to define what is prohibited on Shabbat is 'melacha,' is loosely translated as 'work.' However, the word 'work' as it is used in English can have a different meaning from the word 'melacha.'

The word 'melacha' in the above paragraph from Shemot is used in the discussion of the building of the Mishkan, (Tabernacle) and its vessels while the Israelites were in the wilderness. The Shabbat restrictions are reiterated during this discussion, and it is learned out that the work of creating the Mishkan had to be stopped for Shabbat. From this, our sages concluded that the work forbidden to do on Shabbat is the same as the work done in creating the Mishkan.

The Sages realized thirty-nine categories of work that were required in the construction of the Mishkan and these are what constitute prohibited acts on Shabbat. Everything that we are forbidden to do is derived somehow from these core thirty-nine. For example, digging a hole in the ground to use as a toilet would be derived from melacha #2, plowing. Tying a hammock to a tree is derived from melacha #3, reaping, because we may come to break off a branch. Setting up a tent comes under #34, building. And so on. Here is the full list:

Field Work

1. Sowing 2. Plowing 3. Reaping 4. Binding Sheaves 5. Threshing 6. Winnowing 7. Selecting 8. Grinding 9. Sifting 10. Kneading 11. Baking

Making Material Curtains

12. Shearing Wool 13. Cleaning 14. Combing 15. Dyeing 16. Spinning 17. Stretching the Threads 18. Making Loops 19. Weaving Threads 20. Separating the Threads 21. Tying a Knot 22. Untying a Knot 23. Sewing 24. Tearing

Making Leather Curtains

25. Trapping 26. Slaughtering 27. Skinning 28. Salting 29. Tanning 30. Scraping 31. Cutting

Making the Beams of the Mishkan

32: Writing 33. Erasing

The Putting up and Taking down of the Mishkan

34: Building 35. Breaking Down

The Mishkan's Final Touches

36. Extinguishing a Fire 37. Kindling a Fire 38. Striking the Final Hammer Blow 39. Carrying.

The above thirty-nine are known as the '*Av Melachot*', and from them we end up with thousands of actions prohibited on Shabbat which can make keeping Shabbat incredibly challenging.

Shabbat can be a day of inconvenience and annoyance, or it can be a wonderful and rewarding day. It depends on one's attitude. I prefer not to see things as 'prohibitions', but rather as 'permissions.' During the week, if someone calls me they can be upset if I don't answer their call; but on Shabbat I am permitted to not answer the call. On Shabbat I'm permitted to ignore my email, Facebook, and website comments. On Shabbat I can relax and spend time catching up with family and friends and not worry about work commitments, regardless of what anyone else may think. This is real freedom.

I have travelled through over fifty countries, climbed mountains, trekked through jungles and have always managed to keep Shabbat. To be honest it has not always been easy. There have been times where I've wanted to make a hot bowl of soup, but I can't cook because it is Shabbat. I've had to stop from trekking on perfectly beautiful days. I have had to refrain from repairing backpacks, clothing, and tents when Shabbat afternoon would have been a seemingly perfect opportunity.

At the same time, keeping Shabbat has brought many rewarding experiences, like the time when I hiked solo through the jungles of Papua New Guinea. I learned that the people in the area I was passing through were predominantly Seventh Day Adventist. They had the utmost respect for me because I was, as they put it, 'a Sabbath Keeper.' Many doors were opened and locals welcomed and helped me along the way.

Shabbat has given me an opportunity to reach a deep level of meditation and connection. This occurred at times when I was camped with others and we sang for hours on a Shabbat afternoon to pass the time; or on a Friday night when we lay on the grass gazing up at the stars, and shared powerful stories of great Tzadikim.

When I'm alone, there is plenty of time to practice simply being still and present in the moment. To become aware of everything that is going on around. The sounds of the birds, the frogs, and the raindrops hitting the roof of the tent. The smell of the ocean, a forest, or the aroma of a singular nearby flower. There is so much beauty in all of G-d's creations, from the grand to the minute. When we take the time to become conscious and aware of everything around us, we can see beauty in every cloud, blade of grass, and even a mosquito!

Today we are accustomed to always being in a state of 'doing.' The moment we perceive ourselves as having nothing to do, we get bored and stressed, because we feel we should be doing something. When nothing happens. we fail to realize that the most amazing thing that is continuously happening is that we exist. We can breathe, see, smell, talk, think etc. This is by far more incredible than anything else that could possibly happen - and it is taking place constantly!

I love Shabbat as an opportunity to reflect on all this by taking time to pray and meditate. There is no rush. There is time to reflect on each of the berachot and awaken a sense of deep gratitude and joy.

A large part of why many go camping is to be out in the purity of nature and to re-connect with ourselves, G-d, and the natural universe. We are trying to get away from the noise, the chaos, and pollution of a city where we live. Shabbat therefore is even more so a perfect opportunity to go deeper and find the spiritual space within ourselves. It is not just another night out in the woods of eating roasted marshmallows. It is a uniquely spiritual time when we can tap into something that is not present throughout the rest of the week.

Reach a level of practice and knowhow, and you can comfortably keep Shabbat while camping without experiencing any distress concerning its prohibitions. Then embrace being in the moment with the way things are and let yourself go on the deep spiritual journey that is what Shabbat is really all about.

Acknowledgements

Thank you to Dr. Howard Spielman. Without Howard and his dedication to Shomer Shabbat and kosher Scouting, I would have still found my passion for the outdoors, but Scouting gave me an opportunity to learn about the outdoors while infusing it with Judaism.

Alongside him there were other senior as well as junior leaders who are/were active in Jewish scouting. A special two who come to mind are Daniel Chazen from New Jersey and Harvey Schachter from New York. Thank you for the time you put in organizing many of the activities, from high adventure trips to conclaves, and Jamborees.

Thank you again to my parents who supported me in my Scouting adventure days. For the long drives to bring me to meet up with scouts for a week long canoe or hiking trip. And thank you for paying for scout camp, my hiking boots, backpack etc. until I was able to afford them on my own.

To the many people, too many to list, who have been a part of my outdoor adventures, from canoe trips, backpacking trips, and car camping overnights.

I am thankful to an organization known as DerechHateva in Israel. I worked for a month taking Jewish teens on an outdoor trip across Israel. I learned a lot from the programs director Yael Ukeles about fusing Jewish education and the outdoors, as well as a few important camping skills.

A great big thanks to Klee Benveniste of the Adelaide Hebrew Congregation for her freely-given time working on editing this book, and for her encouragement and creative insights. Also Thank you to Yael Unterman for helping with some of the final editing.

Thank you to Rabbi Whitman for reviewing this content and for writing a meaningful letter to go in the book. Rabbi Whitman's relationship with our family began when he conducted the marriage of my sister Shira and brother in-law some years ago. Today he is a family friend.

About the Author

Rabbi Ben (Binyamin) Tanny has climbed, trekked and camped his way around the world. He has spent Shabbat in the cold and snow on Mt. Aconcagua (South America), in the pouring rain along the Kokoda Trail (Papua New Guinea) and in the blistering heat in the deserts of Australia.

Hailing from an Orthodox family, the second oldest of eleven children, Tanny grew up in Montreal. He attended a Jewish Yeshiva school there, then studied in Australia, where he eventually earned his Semicha (rabbinical ordination).

He began his camping adventures as a participant in a Shomer Shabbat and kosher-keeping Boy Scout troop out of Sharon Massachusetts in the United States. As a teenager, he spent most of his summers sleeping in a tent. He received Eagle Scout in the US and the Chief Scout Award in Canada. The remarkable thing is that he did this all with no compromise to keeping Shabbat or kosher.

He has led hiking/camping trips around the world for Jewish youth and adults, showing them how to not only keep Shabbat while in the outdoors but also how to observe Jewish practice in general.

More about his adventures can be found on his blog at www.travelingrabbi.com. He is available for talks, as a trip guide (to almost anywhere in the world) and to conduct wedding or bar mitzvah ceremonies (also almost anywhere in the world).

CPSIA information can be obtained
at www.ICGtesting.com
Printed in the USA
LVOW10s0145060617
537062LV00035B/1460/P